A SON OF THE RAJ

A Son of The Raj

DR. LESLIE WILLSON. M.C.

The Pentland Press
Edinburgh – Cambridge – Durham – USA

First published in 1996 by
The Pentland Press Ltd
1 Hutton Close,
South Church
Bishop Auckland
Durham

Typeset by Carnegie Publishing, 18 Maynard St, Preston
Printed and bound by Antony Rowe Ltd, Chippenham

*To Marie — A lovely,
Loving, and Loyal Life Partner*

Contents

Acknowledgements

PICTURES FROM *Straight on for Tokyo*, Lt/Col. O.G.W. White
D.S.O.

(1) Two Rivers – Two Bridges
(2) The Three Commanding Officers
(3) Medical Platoon on way to Popa

Maps from *Straight on for Tokyo*.

(1) Burma Campaign
(2) Manipur Road
(3) Tamu Road
(4) Chinwin to Mandalay
(5) Advance to Mandalay
(6) Irrawaddy Crossing
(7) North Central Burma

From *March On* by Norman Havers. M.B.E.

(1) Zubza to Kohima

All maps were drawn by Captain Norman Havers, M.B.E., and reproduced with his permission.

The pictures were reproduced by courtesy and permission of the trustees of the Imperial War Museum.

General reading, revision of events etc.

(1) *Straight on for Tokyo.* by Lt. Col. O.G.W. White, D.S.O.
(2) *March On* by Norman Havers M.B.E.
(3) *The Seige* by Arthur Campbell, M.C.
(4) *Beyond the Chinwin* by Major Bernard Fergusson, D.S.O. O.B.E.
(5) *Chindits* by Richard Rhodes James.
(6) *Wingate's Raiders* by Charles J. Rolo.
(7) *Elephant Bill* by Lt. Col. J.H. Williams, O.B.E.
(8) *The Jungle is Neutral* by F. Spencer Chapman, D.S.O.
(9) *The Mauritius Command* by Patrick O'Brien.
(10) *Kidnapped & Catriona.* by Robert Louis Stevenson.
(11) *Kohima* by Arthur Swinson.

Preface

To my readers

I HOPE YOU ENJOY MY AUTOBIOGRAPHY, one covering a wide range of happenings, geographically, culturally, socially, militarily, etc. You will, I hope, find it not only lively, but also absorbing, and entertaining.

I have attempted to give you a reasonably honest account of happenings as they impinged on my life over the years. The words 'reasonably honest' have been deliberately chosen, for who can swear that his own narrative is one hundred per cent accurate? Should anyone find in my account, serious errors of commission or omission I would be grateful to receive constructive suggestions. Especially so, in my account of the Kohima-Imphal-Mandalay-Mt. Popa part of the Campaign, relating to my personal experience in this theatre of war. It makes no pretence to be a complete account, but I truly believe it, within its limitations, to be an accurate one. The occasional absence of articles, prepositions, and even the odd verb is not accidental, The style was copied from my diary, written in haste, just after the time of action. Something surely would be lost in too formal a transcription.

I apologise for the quality of the photographs. These are photostats of faded original 'Positives', many over 50 years of age. It is a wonder that they came out at all!!

Without further ado, I recommend you move on to Chapter One. 'Early Years'.

Early Years

MY BIRTH CERTIFICATE STATED 23 FEBRUARY 1918, Bombay, together with the names of my parents, and significant witnesses.

It gave no indication of future events, nor unexpected, and sometimes, dangerous happenings, nor of exotic places like Mauritius, Burma, Malaya and Java. It failed to mention Western countries such as England, Scotland, Ireland and Australia.

My story begins in Bombay and follows over the years, adventures, some hazardous, in many parts of the world. Little can I remember of my early years in Bombay with my Father and Mother.

I can recall conversing in Urdu with my 'AYAH'. She taught me the only language she knew, during my baby years. This was the accepted custom in those days, the Ayah (Indian Nurse) taking over the daily management of the Sahib and Memsahib's children during their 'nappy and post-nappy years'.

In this era, dysentery, typhoid and other tropical diseases were all too prevalent, consequent of limited public health measures and the absence of antibiotic medication.

At 4 years of age I contracted dysentery of a virulent strain and nearly died, leaving me debilitated with much loss of weight. The doctors advised a long convalescence in a favourable climate. Mother wished to take me to Grandmother's home in Mauritius, besides, 'the sea trip would do him good.'

Sometime during the voyage I was 'missing', searches were organised to no avail.

Query, Boy overboard?

Always an excellent climber, (You little monkey), I was eventually located some 50 feet above the deck, in the Crow's nest, admiring the bow waves, and the flying fish. My recent illness saved me from the spanking I richly deserved.

The family home at Quatre Bornes in Mauritius consisted of a large house with wide surrounding verandahs together with an adjacent pavilion standing in some two acres of ground. Best of all, trees!! Mango, guava, letchi, peach, and banana, all for the climbing. Grandma, now widowed, had many members of her large family living with her, sons George, John, and Denis, and daughters, Evelyn, Ivy, and Bertha, together with her grandsons, Roy and myself. A warm, friendly family.

Grandma had a staff of cook, maid and gardener to tend her large establishment. The Creole staff had numerous children who were usually found playing somewhere in and around the large grounds. Roy and I often joined them in their games, frequently bare footed for better climbing. In play, and laughter, they taught us their native Creole. French, we learned at school, English, at home. By nine years of age, we were fluently trilingual. All three languages are freely spoken in Mauritius, originally a French Colony, but taken over during the many wars with France. (Vide: *The Mauritius Command*, Fontana Publications).

When the season of the year was suitable, a stay at the seaside was arranged, accommodation, a government bungalow, which Uncle George's position as a Senior Government Officer warranted. The bungalow at 'Tamarin' was situated close to the sea, with large verandahs from where one could see and hear the incoming waves breaking over the reef and the shore. Old Lionel, the caretaker of the bungalow, lived close by with his wife and children, natural playmates for Roy and myself. Large banyan trees fringed the area, their long trailing vines seeking the soil, inviting us to grasp, run and swing from them. At low tide the reef bared itself with many residual pools, in which fish and octopi were trapped until freed by the incoming tide. Using homemade spears, Roy and I frequently sought such prey and often brought home several varieties of fish and an occasional octopus. Sun dried octopus tentacles, chopped into small pieces, and salted can be chewed like plug tobacco, and when curried have a taste which can be acquired. Under-cooking results in trying to chew pieces resembling India-rubber!! We made many such stays at 'Tamarin', so called, because of its many trees of that name, a lovely area with miles of unspoiled beaches. (1925). During one of our stays at the bungalow a tragedy was narrowly averted. Roy and I were playing with Lionel's children, when we came across his 12-bore shotgun. How is it that boys rather than girls, have a knack of finding things dangerous to others and to themselves? I picked up the shotgun, heavy for an eight year old, and was about to point it at Roy, saying 'Bang you're dead,' as in cowboy play. Something, perhaps my Guardian Angel, (I must have one to have survived to write this) prompted me to divert my aim to a nearby tree. I pressed the trigger 'Click', the second, 'Bang', the kick-recoil bowling me over, and the buck shot scarring the tree trunk. Better to draw a veil over what followed, never since, war years excepted, have I ever pointed a gun or pistol at anyone.

A further episode of potential disaster followed some time later. Roy and I were climbing to retrieve a particularly lush cluster of mangoes, something we did frequently and with ease of much practice, when a branch I was grasping broke free from the trunk. Down I plunged, a fall of some 20 feet, (Mango trees grow tall), head first into a large underlying bush with final connection of head onto rocky soil. Dazed, I staggered up, put hand to head, and felt some moisture. 'You're bleeding,' shouted Roy, and so I was. Hearing the commotion, out raced Aunt Bertha, and moments later I was being examined by our local Doctor. Portable X-rays were not then generally available, but a clinical examination revealed no serious damage, although a sizeable scalp wound was present. Wound cleaned, injection of anti-tetanus given, head bandaged, I was driven home, and put to bed. Today, I can touch and feel a round depression the size of a shilling on my scalp and realise that the bony 'outer-table' of my skull had been 'dented' at the time. Scar tissue had replaced the denuded skin, a narrow shave indeed!!

The description of life at 'Quatre Bornes' would be incomplete without Jack and Togo. Jack medium sized, black, with odd white marking, was the family's watch-dog. In those days Jack had little to do, since the local population was law-abiding and the family well respected. Jack was not a vicious dog, a lazy hound really, but he had, over the years, bitten every one of Grandma's large family. I still have the scar on my cheek as a memento of Jack.

The family loved Jack and accepted those occasional lapses which also included the postman, and tradesmen. Today, Jack would not have lasted beyond his first two bites before being put down. People seemed more tolerant towards animals in those days.

The biting act was usually as follows:

Jack would be asleep in one of his lairs, when someone, not previously briefed, would attempt to pat him. He would resent being awakened, and retaliate with a sharp 'nip'. He never chased them nor gave more than an initial 'friendly nip,' at any time.

Alas, old age caught up with Jack; in sorrow, we buried him with a silent prayer. Togo was smaller and of a placid nature. One could pat him any time, even pull his ears with impunity. Roy and I came to love him and he became our special friend. Togo lived to the ripe old age of 18 years, spent happily with the family. Alas, I was never to see him again after leaving Mauritius. He had long passed away by the time I was able to return.

Life continued to be interesting and pleasant, fortunately, with no further potential disasters. Roy and I, with Auntie Evelyn, (Roy's mother) were soon to return to Bombay.

CHAPTER TWO

Back to Bombay

WHEN I REACHED THE AGE OF SOME 9 YEARS, it was decided that Roy and I should return to Bombay with Aunt Evelyn to join Mum and Dad. The sea trip was uneventful and our reception warm. It was nice to feel we had two homes as it were.

Roy and I were enrolled at John Connon School, the Junior school of 'Cathedral High' and made the daily trip accompanied by, and under the watchful eye of our 'Hamal', one of Dad's reliable male servants.

I cannot recall any major events or crises during the two to three years at school in Bombay, except perhaps on one occasion.

'Missing' for some hours, I was eventually found, some two miles away, on the beach, sitting in the 'driving seat' of a sand-car. This I had built with wet sand and the steering wheel from flotsam. My Father's keys formed part of the car's ignition. No prizes offered on the outcome of this little escapade!!

Trip to Patiala

Some weeks later mother received a letter from a long separated school friend, now married with husband and two sons. They were now in Patiala, some 880 miles north of Bombay. Patiala was an independent Indian State with its own court and Government. Mother and I were invited to spend a few weeks with them. The ladies wished to see each other again, talk over old times and catch up with local gossip. The train journey was interesting and long in duration, watching the different villages and the country-side glide by.

At Patiala we were fortunate in witnessing a real 'Levee', a Royal birthday occasion.

The Royal Mounted Troops were resplendent in colourful uniforms with lances and swords glittering in the bright sunlight. The horses were magnificent animals, appropriately adorned for the occasion. it was an inspiring performance from both men and horses, carried out with zest, precision, and excellent horsemanship.

About this time the wrestling champion of India, and a great favourite with his followers, was Gama. Henry and I were of an age, we made a wrestling ring by digging up the hard soil, with much raking to smooth the surface. There we fought out many bouts, Henry as Gama and I as his latest opponent. We had fun and quite a few bruises, spurred on by the cheers of the Indian servants and their children who had entered into the spirit of the sport.

My parents

My Father was born in London County in 1892, his Father an accountant and his Mother a teacher. At 16 years of age he was apprenticed to a major shipping firm and soon posted as a Junior Officer on one of the company's sailing ships. Over the next few years my Father served in windjammers and clippers plying to India and the Americas. The long haul around the Cape to India through the Roaring Forties was particularly hazardous and trying. For weeks on end all aboard had to endure wind, rain and cold in 'rounding the Cape'

Nothing could be kept dry and hot meals were a rarity. Despite these adverse conditions my Father survived and managed to study the many aspects of seamanship and to learn from the experienced Ship's Officers, navigation, ships' lore, etc.

By examinations, taken whilst at home ports, my Father obtained his Maritime Certificates from Junior to Senior Ship's Officer, and finally his Master's Certificate. About this time he transferred from Sail to Steam joining the British-India Line, (the 'B.I.'). One of the many ports of call was Mauritius, where on shore leave my Father first met my Mother and became engaged. She was the daughter of the British magistrate of Quatre Bornes, and Granddaughter of the Reverend Adolphus Vaudin of Sark. It was months before the ship's return to Mauritius and the opportunity came for them to be married.

Soon afterwards my Father joined the Bombay Pilot Service and established a firm base and house for his bride.

All Pilots were ex-ships' Officers, most of them holding a Master's Certificate which entitled them to captain a ship.

Over the ensuing years, through personal, navigational, and administrative ability coupled with a fluency in Urdu and sound staff relationship, my Father rose from Pilot to senior Pilot, Dockmaster to Harbour Master, and finally to the top post of the Deputy Conservator. This placed him in charge of all shipping entering and leaving the Port of Bombay. This, a major world port, was to play a vital part in harbouring and replenishing Allied Convoys in south-east Asia during World War II.

I am very proud of my Father. Amongst other things, he achieved the position of Deputy Conservator in the face of strong competition, including from Officers of the Royal Navy. I understand that my Father was the first Merchant Navy Officer to be so appointed. (Dad served as a ship's Officer during World War I.) On the social side, I can recall many evenings when Dad's fellow pilots and their wives, were invited to dinner, served with quiet dignity by our turbanned butler. After dinner, in those pre-television days, everyone was expected to contribute to the evening's entertainment. Conversation was lively and far ranging, despite the inevitable 'shop talk'. Most of those present could sing, play an instrument, or relate a good joke or two, censored for the occasion.

My Father in his youth was a regular member of a Church Choir of some standing. He possessed a fine baritone voice. He

My Parents' Wedding

had always been interested in music and taught himself to play the piano and the Church organ. Mother had a pleasant soft voice, soprano. She and Dad sang many a pleasant duet with Dad at the piano. Mother's favourite was the 'Londonderry Air', which often brought a tear to the listener's eye. Mum and Dad were a lovely pair, sadly I saw so little of them, consequent of events, world and domestic, beyond our control.

As an expatriate British Officer Dad was entitled to home leave of some five months for every 3–4 years of service. His leave having fallen due, by ship in a comfortable cabin, we steamed away for England in 1932.

My cousin Roy, at the age of 18 years, volunteered for war service, and embarked with many others to join up in Bombay. Sad to relate, their ship was torpedoed with loss of Roy, passengers and crew, within a few hours of leaving Mauritius.

CHAPTER THREE

England and Scotland

O^{N ARRIVAL IN ENGLAND} Dad rented an apartment near Croyden from where we made several trips to London. Mother went shopping, Dad and I visited the Tower of London, the Science Museum, and many places of interest.

I found the Science Museum fascinating, especially the working models. For the price of a penny in the slot one could activate and demonstrate their use. After running out of pennies my Father decided it was time to move on, we had already spent some hours there. Only later did Dad tell me that we had only covered the ground floor, there was plenty more to see!!

Academically, the local English school provided some continuity of education for me. I was comfortable with English, French, and Geography, but found Mathematics more than a little tricky. This brought to the fore the main question, one faced by all expatriate parents – where to educate an 11 year old son or daughter? At this critical age a good all round education was essential, it was generally considered that this could best be obtained in Britain. Discussions followed with my Auntie Aggie, who with her four children, all older than I, was resident in Scotland, near the Naval base at Rosyth in the County of Fife. In short, I became one of the Mackay family with my Aunt and cousins when my parents returned to India. My Aunt Aggie was widowed and she was determined to do the best for her four children and myself. Her husband had been Director of Education in Fiji and Trinidad whilst in the Colonial Service. She was kind but firm, and amongst other attributes proved to be a natural nurse when any of us fell ill. I became very fond of her.

The local school was of high academic standard, the Scots placing great stress on a good education. The pupils however were rather rougher than I had so far encountered. As a new boy, and a 'Sassenach' at that, I came in for some rough treatment from time to time. However, like the famous pocket-battleship, what I could not sink I could outrun!!

The Maths sessions in class were particularly interesting and instructive, the first ten minutes of which being spent on active, mental Arithmetic. The pupils, after years of such practice, were faster than computers in their replies. Questions and answers buzzed across the classroom like angry bees – a newcomer had no chance at all.

A year later, Doreen, the eldest of the family, had reached University age and had passed her 'Matric' with sister May only a year behind. Aunt Aggie therefore moved the family to Edinburgh, to a comfortable apartment in Marchmont overlooking the Braid Hills so that we all in turn could attend Edinburgh University.

Edinburgh is a lovely city, my favourite, along with Brisbane. It is mellow in summer with days of bright sunshine but can turn bitter in the winter, especially when icy winds blow in from the Firth of Forth and the North Sea! Of special interest is the Old Town, the original 'Auld Reekie', well described by Robert Louis Stevenson in *Kidnapped* and *Catriona*.

The Old Town's main street, the Royal Mile, winds its way from Edinburgh Castle, sitting solidly on its lofty massive rock formation, to the grounds of Holyrood Palace. During their visits to Scotland this is where the Royal Family resides. At other times, Holyrood Palace is open to visitors, under benevolent supervision and payment of a modest fee.

The Royal Mile is flanked by 2–3 storey stone houses of antiquity. Amongst them is the house of John Knox, with its solid wooden door, inches thick, and its attached 'door-nail' to herald its visitors. The 'door-nail' is of course, the father of the modern knocker. It was made of solid iron, curved and heavy, and resulted in a single loud sound with no bounce on striking the door. Hence, it is said, sprang the saying, 'as dead as a door-nail'.

Of interest, also, is the expression 'Gardey-loo', a corruption of the French *Gardez-vous*. This is stated to be the warning shout given by the long gone inhabitants of the upper storeys along the way, prior to emptying a loaded pot through the window onto the street. Those walking below had little time to jump clear! Needless to say, this habit dates back some two to three centuries.

Some distance away, at the top of the street leading from the Mound, is the statue of Greyfriars Bobby, a little terrier. In their day, Bobby and his Master were well known locally, and always together. On the death of his master, Bobby sat on guard over his master's grave, staying there in all weathers, leaving briefly to be fed daily by kind neighbours then returning to his post.

Bobby's devotion caught the attention of the local people, resulting in a bronze statue of the dog being struck and erected for all to see after his death.

New Town is the modern Edinburgh with wide streets and imposing buildings gracing the city centre. Princes Street extends for a mile, from the old solid North British Hotel at its eastern end to the Caledonian Hotel at the western end.

One could say that Princes Street is the modern counterpart of the old Royal Mile. On its Castle side, lie the Princes Street Gardens which extend along its full length.

The Castle, sitting high on its rocky perch, dominates the scene. Many a time as a schoolboy had I visited its Banqueting Hall, with its fine collection of armour, claymores, and early muskets. From the castle ramparts one could view the whole of Princes Street and, far beyond, the waters of the Firth of Forth. Curiously enough, it was some 20 years later, as a visitor from Australia, that I signed the visitors' book.

On the area adjacent to the ramparts were many old cannons,

the most famous being 'Mons Meg', a massive one which once fired a ball of some 20 inches in diameter. Close by were a row of modern guns in a neat semi-circle, muzzles pointing over the city, and not accessible to the public. Once daily one was fired at precisely one o'clock to denote the time – 'The One O'clock Gun'.

The gardens cover many acres, with walkways neatly trimmed and a profusion òf flowers in season. Of special interest to the tourist is the Floral Clock, some 12 feet in diameter. The clock's whole face is made up of different coloured flowers with distinctive time figures. The massive clock hands have small shrubs implanted on their upper surfaces. The floral clock keeps good time, controlled and operated from an underlying stone vault.

The most striking feature on the way along Princes Street is the Scott's Monument, a memorial to Sir Walter Scott, of literary fame. Built of stone, of beautiful architecture, the structure stretches skywards, not unlike the Eiffel Tower in Paris. For a moderate fee one is permitted to climb the enclosed stairs to view the City from aloft. Close by in the gardens are the Art Galleries, well designed, of stone structure and pleasing to the eye. Many visual treasures are housed there. The Galleries participate in the annual Edinburgh Festival. On the opposite side of Princes Street are many stately shops with all sorts of merchandise available for sale to the tourist.

At its west end was Binns, a multiple store with a well patronised dining room and coffee lounge, a favourite meeting place on a Saturday morning, especially for University students when they could afford it!!! My Aunt Aggie's apartment, like others built in this era, was of solid stone structure with large bay windows, large rooms, and high ceilings. It was situated on the 3rd floor (Top) and overlooked a large private ground, beyond which we could see the Braid Hills in all their many moods. Electronics were not around when the apartment was built. To ring the bell there was a large polished brass knob beside the front door. When pulled firmly and strongly this activated a bell in the upstairs apartment. One then pulled a similar knob, which via concealed wires and pulleys, opened the downstairs door. No voice nor television contact with potential visitor was available, but then one could simply lean out of the bay window and view them first hand!

Schooldays

The Mackays did well, Doreen and May each passing and obtaining their M.A. with Honours. Ian obtained his C.A. in accountancy, and Gordon his M.B.Ch.B. in medicine.

I attended Craigend Park School for the next five years, a private school with many extras in the curriculum. Better than average at class studies and good at sports I gained my First Fifteen Rugby cap and two swimming diving medals.

I made several good friends at school including John, whose friendship lasted throughout the years until his death a few years ago. We were in the same rugby team, he in the forwards, myself less burly but fleet of foot, as wing three-quarter. Apart from weekly practices and cross-country runs, we played rival schools every Saturday morning, rain or shine. I still recall one such match during the depths of winter, played on a frozen pitch. During the game snow began to fall, getting heavier by the minute and driven by a moderate gale. After ten minutes of such cruel exposure the opposing team fled the field, leaving us the winners by default!

I have often wondered, in hindsight, how we schoolboys survived such conditions, perhaps the resilience of youth.

I enjoyed my years at Craigend and in due course obtained my Matric for entry to Edinburgh University.

CHAPTER FOUR

Edinburgh (1937–40)

THE YEAR 1937 ARRIVED AND WITH IT MY PARENTS, home on leave from India. Mum and Dad came to Edinburgh and rented an apartment not far from Aunt Aggie's and close to the Meadows.

The Meadows was a park of many acres, with several paths crossing its wide area. A mile walk brought me to the Medical School and the Royal Infirmary. How many thousands of times did I traverse on foot this pleasant walk in 'thunder, lightning, and in rain'! It was very nice being with my parents during my first term at Medical School.

All too soon their leave was over and Aunt Aggie and I waved them goodbye on Waverley Station as the Flying Scotsman bore them away, its engine enshrouded in clouds of steam. I returned to the Mackay ménage, now only three strong. Doreen had taken a secretarial post in England and Ian had joined the Colonial Audit Service and had been posted to Accra, in West Africa.

May was teaching at school locally, prior to joining the Colonial Education Service and being posted to East Africa, Gordon in the final year at Medical school, and I in my first year. The opening week in Medical school was taken up with registering for the various courses in first year anatomy, physics, chemistry, botany, zoology, etc. and the paying of the relevant fees.

Prior to my parents' homecoming I had made out a list of fees in some detail, which covered the five years of the medical courses.

I discussed with my Father my wish to study medicine and requested his financial help in undertaking this long and arduous course. Dad looked over this formidable list of fees with some care then said, 'I think I can provide it for you, but why medicine? I could be of help if you took up something to do with the sea, but I have no knowledge, nor influence in the medical field.'

This was not an easy question to answer, there were multiple reasons which I attempted to explain; the most potent factor was probably the influence of my cousin Gordon. Over the first four years of his medical studies we had often discussed the ongoing aspects of the medical course, the interesting diagnosis of the day and the personalities of his many teachers.

This had kindled my interest and I had watched from the students' gallery some of the famous surgeons of the day operating, and listening to their comments. I had also, from the gallery, listened to and observed some of the medical 'greats' taking their out-patient sessions and was highly impressed. I began to feel that eventually, if I studied hard enough, I could become a good doctor.

The Anatomy course consisted of lectures, demonstrations and dissection, with ongoing exams. Imagine the shock of one's first visit to the dissecting room – a long large room smelling strongly of formalin with many zinc covered tables, on each of which was a naked corpse!

We put on our white protective coats, opened our individual dissecting instruments bought at our own expense, containing scissors, scalpel, forceps, etc. and stood in stunned silence looking at each other. One of the doctor-demonstrators came up to us, eight students to a cadavre, and said, 'Well?' We gazed at him in silence. He then allocated us as follows, two students to each limb. We duly took up our allotted places and opened our dissecting manuals for advice.

Who was going to make the first incision? Observing our hesitation the demonstrator came over and made four wide incisions, pointing out the main exposed structures, and said, 'Dissect, and expose these vessels and nerves, I'll be back to inspect your efforts.'

We survived the first and subsequent days. Each term we rotated to dissect a different portion of the body. By the end of the second year, we were proficient in dissection and had acquired a surprising knowledge of the human anatomy, which would stand us in good stead for future surgical operative work. Our first medical year consisted of some 200 students, a small proportion being women, together with a sizeable number of students from the Empire, now the Commonwealth!

With students from Scotland, Ireland, Wales, and overseas, we made up a cosmopolitan group. By the end of the year we knew each other by sight and soon by name.

We got on well together and made lasting friendships, James, Reg, and Bob being mine. Studies apart, some form of recreation was essential to compliment the approaching 5 years of academic 'grind'.

Not being particularly 'Arty', I opted for two of the many sporting activities available, joining the University Boxing Club, and Sports' Club. The former functioned for the two winter terms, the latter for the summer term. In addition I joined the 'O.T.C.' (Officers Training Corps), which had regular parades and a camp of a fortnight at the year's end.

Towards the end of our first year a special event was staged in the McEwan Hall to mark the achievements of members of the various socio-sporting clubs. The members of the Boxing Club arranged a brief, action packed presentation, two bouts each of three one minute rounds, with light and heavyweight alternating bouts. Being in his lightweight division, Tipping, our boxing Captain chose me to box against him in this demonstration. We practised and perfected a few special boxing moves to enhance our performance and to keep our audience on its toes; it went well. Afterwards, in the changing room, on removing my boxing singlet, an 'Aertex' open weave, I found that Tipping had inflicted a temporary tattoo of the weave on to my chest. For a lightweight he had a solid punch in each hand!

The end of the first medical year came and with it our examination results. We had had many ongoing exams throughout the year but this was the final big one, pass, or fail the year. Thankfully I passed.

Holidays began, and forward to the 'O.T.C.' camp, held this year at Turnberry on the west coast. It was the month of July, and thank heavens we were granted a whole fortnight of sunshine. Rain and a tented camp made poor companions. Parades, kit inspections, lectures, demonstrations and early reveille were orders of the day. My fellow cadets, eight of us to a tent, coped with it all and so did I. Except for guard duties, the evening were free, but back by 11p.m. (23.00 hours) from the nearby town, a walk of some 3 miles. We ended up physically fit by the end of our fortnight's camp.

This was to be the last such camp for many years, the threat of approaching war required the Officers, and N.C.O.s running the camp for more serious duties and our tents and equipment were needed as well.

Second Year

Thank heavens the many primary scientific subjects lay behind us now. Our main studies for the next 12 months, were Anatomy and Physiology, a major reduction in the number of subjects. Both subjects included hours of practical work. Dissection in Anatomy, with frequent ongoing tests by the demonstrators, experimental laboratory work in physiology, requiring full description and a full write-up of each case. Thankful for small mercies, you say? I agree.

Adjacent to the Medical School and Union Buildings was the Pollock Gymnasium.

Pollock Gymnasium

Here Colonel Campbell, D.S.O., Director of Physical Education of Edinburgh University, offered many courses to tempt students to become and remain fit. He believed, and proved, that students physically fit could study better than when unfit. I had already discovered that often, whilst studying in the Union library between classes, my chin would crash on to my chest to awaken me!!

Nothing I was reading was being retained, a form of mental fatigue had set in. So to the gym I trailed, to put in a half hour with Tom, our gym master, and his class. Following a good work-out, a hot shower, a brisk rub down, now wide awake I could study and retain what I was reading. The total time involved was only an hour.

Some weeks later Tom suggested that I combine my gym visits with Colonel Campbell's special programme leading to a Certificate in Physical Proficiency. This course involved achieving a wide ranging set of physical standards designed to bring out the best in one.

The course was flexible to suit the availability of the individual student. It was good fun with some hard work, and not unduly time-consuming. I still value my certificate. Mention must be made of our University Union, a unique institution I believe, in that it was controlled and run by a committee of students. Under their charge was a Resident Manager and many daily visiting staff. The committee consisted of six members and a President who were elected annually by their fellow students.

The Union was a large, three storey stone building, with a basement in the old style and a covered space at the rear where students could park their bicycles. Few students at that time owned their own car; of over 200 members of my year, only 5 were so fortunate.

Within the building, centrally heated, a blessing during the Scottish winter, were many rooms for both study and recreation.

It sported a Fives court, four billiard tables, showers, toilets and baths, library, bar and dining room. A cafeteria supplied cakes, tea and coffee.

Many a time my friends and I sat in a group, gazing mournfully into our coffee cups after sitting a particularly difficult exam, wondering how we had fared. On the top floor was the Debating Hall, a very large room with high Cathedral ceilings, a surrounding gallery and a large area of smooth oaken floor. You've guessed it!! Every Saturday evening from 7.00–11.30 p.m. during the academic year, was held the 'Union Palais'. This was an informal dance with a 'real' Jazz band. For payment of a modest fee and production of Matriculation Card, any student was eligible to attend.

Also current was a standing invitation to the young ladies of Atholl Crescent, students of the School of Domestic Science. These young ladies came to study from all parts of Scotland and many other countries, and were boarded in hostels, some in proximity to our Union. They attended the 'Palais' in groups of three or four and were soon swept up in the dance. They were graceful and attractive. Nor surprisingly, many long term relationships were so formed and not a few marriages followed their graduation.

A few weeks into the first term of second year I met an attractive Scottish lass, with auburn hair, a nice figure, and a bubbly sense of humour. We met one Saturday evening at the 'Palais', she arrived in the company of several fellow students.

'May I have the pleasure of this dance?'

We ventured on to the dance floor to the tune of a foxtrot, she was light of foot and easily followed my steps, we danced the evening through. As we neared 11.30 p.m. like Cinderella she said, 'I must be going home now.' 'May I walk you home?' She laughed, 'Only if you don't mind walking 20 miles.' We compromised, hurrying to put her safely on the last bus home.

We met regularly, usually at the 'Palais', but sometimes took in a picture or a play. Some spare afternoons we met for cakes and coffee at Martin's, a favourite student rendezvous situated opposite the Royal Infirmary. As the year neared its end we both needed to prepare for our respective exams and saw less and less of each other. Following the long summer vacation, we drifted apart and so ended my first real romance. *C'est la vie*!!!

With the second year of Medicine now passed and completed, the clouds of war were fast gathering in Europe and finally burst on 3 September 1939. Enemy paratroops were expected to be dropped in vital areas to sabotage and to soften-up things prior to the invasion. There was no hysteria, only a realistic anticipation of events. The Home Guard was formed to guard essential areas and to delay the enemy until arrival of the nearest Army Units. I found myself promoted to the rank of Corporal, on the strength of my O.T.C. experience.

In 'khaki' uniform, (battle dress), bayonet in scabbard, carrying an ancient bolt-action rifle, (not even a trusty 'Lee-Enfield') in relays we took up our defensive positions. Now, knowing my way around infantry weapons following my Army service, I would assess that our detachment would have been wiped out in seconds, rather than minutes. Fortunately the enemy did not come but our part-time service helped morale, ours if not theirs!!

In preparation for things to come I was taken on during the vacation as a 'student-helper' at the 'S.O.P.D.' (Surgical Outpatients' Department) of the Royal Infirmary. This led to a variety of tasks, taking off and replacing plasters, assisting surgeons and anaesthetists, lifting patients on and off the trolleys etc. An extra pair of willing hands you might say, but it was good experience.

Third Year

Third Year now commenced with multiple subjects, including pathology, bacteriology, Materia Medica, general medicine and surgery. Best of all was our introduction into the wards of the Edinburgh Royal Infirmary. We were allocated in small groups to one of its many wards, medical and surgical. We were under the clinical instruction of such 'Greats' as Professor Sir Stanley Davidson, Professor Sir Derrick Dunlop, and many others.

In surgery our 'Chiefs' were Professor Learmonth, Frank E. Jardine, and other famous surgeons. We attended our allocated wards daily at 9 a.m. going first to the war 'side-room' where, seated, we received the clinical instructions of the day. We were then shepherded into the ward for a ward round, with the Consultant or his assistant, and came face to face with *real* patients.

We had to endure questions on clinical findings, thus – 'Put your stethoscope there, what do you hear?'

Or, 'Palpate this patient's abdomen, what do you feel?'

'The liver man, the liver, can't you feel it?'

I must say the patients were very patient indeed, they seemed to regard this intrusion into their privacy as a necessary part of the ward routine – full marks to them.

Each new term brought a change of ward and different teachers, from third year to fifth year (inclusive), giving experience of a wide varieties of disorders and teachers. We also built up, on the way, a little self-confidence, shattered initially when surrounded by fellow students, patients and teachers we faced questions we could not answer.

About halfway through the year, as Secretary of the Boxing Club I received a letter from the Wing Commander of a nearby 'R.A.F.' base inviting us to spar with their boxing team. This was to be an exhibition match to entertain the 'Troops'. We could scarcely refuse such an offer and having selected our team we duly arrived, were welcomed and shown to our changing rooms. Came my turn to enter the ring and face my opponent, friendly matches are rarely so!

We touched gloves, retreated a few steps, and it was on. He came at me like a whirlwind, fists flying and full of beans. My friend James in the audience said later, 'I thought you were a "gonner"!' My guard up, weaving and ducking, with agile foot-work I avoided most of his blows, taking the remainder on forearms and gloves. Round one definitely went to him!!

Round Two began at a lesser pace, he was beginning to tire, a fighter not a boxer, with little experience in the art of footwork and defence. Now I was able to turn the tide, and attack, using a long fast straight left to the face, to discourage his advances and a right hook, or right cross, whenever an opening presented – my round.

Round Three, my opponent now very tired, I had to box very gently to keep things alive.

The meeting was successful, we were entertained afterwards and plied with tea and cakes before returning safely home.

Third year now passed and completed and the summer vacation ahead, onward to Peel Emergency Hospital in Selkirkshire, with a small group of fellow students. The general call-up of doctors to the Armed Services was now being felt on the civilian side (1941), and such help as we could offer was welcomed.

Peel Hospital was one of many E.M.S. Hospitals thrown up in country areas in anticipation of heavy civilian and military casu-alties.

The main building was a massive stone structure over a century old, multi-storeyed and multi-roomed, built like a castle, which housed medical, nursing and administrative staff. In its spacious grounds were built many pavilion style wards with operating theatres, laboratories, etc. Clinical work went on apace, we helped, we were taught as we went along, we learned.

All was not work, however, being somewhat isolated in the countryside we made our own recreation.

Weekend tennis matches, the summer was unusually kind, mixed doubles with doctors, nurses and medical students participating, were frequently arranged. This was followed by a tea and cake session on the lawns, with a general social intermingling. Towards the end of our stay at Peel, a review was produced by the staff-nurses, doctors and students all taking part.

Surprising talent was found, musical, vocal and comedy. Called the 'Peeloptimists', the show was given to patients and staff, it was a great success.

Fourth Year

Fourth Year now with subjects including medicine and surgery, midwifery and gynaecology, public health, forensic medicine. Also our daily ward rounds conducted at the Edinburgh Royal. The pace was not now so hectic, there was time for study and revision. I was able to read ahead of the lecturers, especially in midwifery, thus finding it easier to follow, and record the lectures.

As an essential part of the midwifery course all students were required to conduct a minimum number of normal deliveries under supervision. This was arranged during the vacation, the students being housed in a University hostel close to the maternity wards. An alternative avenue revealed itself, it appeared that the Rotunda Hospital in Dublin had long had such a 'live-in' arrangement for their students, both under- and post-graduate.

A mutual appreciation of each others' high standards in this field had led to students from Edinburgh being permitted to undertake their practical midwifery course at the Rotunda Hospital.

Not having been to Ireland and wishing to do so I investigated this possibility. After much form filling and interview permission was obtained, not so easy in wartime with its security enforcements. Within days of obtaining such permission, I found myself on a ferry crossing the Irish Sea, in company of other students heading for the Rotunda Hospital, Dublin.

CHAPTER FIVE

Dublin (1941)
The Rotunda Hospital

THE STUDENT HOSTEL WAS NEW, four storeyed and adjacent to the maternity and labour wards. Each student had his/her room furnished with bed, cupboard, chest of drawers, desk and chair, wash basin.

Having registered for the course, I unpacked and later went down to dinner, sitting with the others at a long community table in the style of King Arthur's Court, with the Assistant Master, at the head. Compared with the rationing of wartime British meals, the fare was excellent.

Next morning we assembled (I nearly said paraded), in the main lecture room, where we were given full instructions relating to the courses, the need for strictest asepsis etc. During the next few days, scrubbed up, hands and forearms plunged deep into pool of Dettol solution, dried, gloved and capped, I delivered my first baby under the eagle eye of the Sister-in-charge, surely a milestone in one's life. Following several such deliveries and, remember, after a full year of midwifery lecture and exams, I was allowed to join a team of four other students, on 'stand by' for a delivery on the district. This was carried out in the patient's own home.

Each student had his/her own maternity bag (à la midwife), containing sterile swabs, packs and towels, abdominal binders, safety pins, artery forceps and scissors (to clamp and cut the umbilical cord). And for the baby, a sucker to aspirate mucus from his/her throat, and ½% silver nitrate solution in dropping bottle, for the baby's eyes to eliminate possible infection.

Each team was on standby for 24 hours, and members were not permitted to leave the hospital during this time until called to 'District'. The bell was sounded when the call came, we grabbed our maternity bags, piled into the hospital car and rushed to our destination. Water was already on the boil in the traditional manner!

We met the Mother-to-be, made a careful examination and found her ready for delivery. She had had several children and could probably have instructed us as to what had to be done.

First-timers, *primigravidae*, went to the Rotunda Hospital for their deliveries, and rightly so. Following our successful delivery of a baby boy, we made the mother comfortable and after checking the baby's condition once more, we bade goodday but not good-bye. The students on district worked as a team, the one performing the actual delivery had to record all relevant findings on a special chart. Next day and for a week afterwards, the team paid daily visits, recording the patient's blood pressure, pulse rate, temperature, height of uterus fundus, etc.

Any abnormality found in mother, or child was reported without delay to the doctor on duty at the Rotunda. At the end of the 10 days, I bade our good lady farewell and handed in her chart for inspection, and for the records. Altogether an efficient arrangement with minimal disturbance to the mother and her family.

Second week at the Rotunda

I was passing the foyer when I saw a small group of young men and women students from the Royal College of Surgeons, Dublin, signing their names on the student register on the official notice board.

Across a crowded room I saw 'Her', as she signed her name and walked away.

After all these years it is difficult for me to do justice to my first impression.

She was simply, but tastefully dressed, with hair a dark brown, parted in the middle, lovely mien and a trim feminine figure. As she strolled out of the room I admired her walk. I felt I must see her again. I examined the notice board, and found her name to be Marie. Her signature was clear against her name, written with a rare classical flourish.

Next morning I went to the students' sitting-room to look at the morning paper. She was bending over the fire, poker in hand, trying to stir some life into it. At close range I looked into a pair of big brown eyes, set in a lovely face, and felt my heart miss a beat!! 'Good morning,' I greeted her and sat on the arm of the sofa, watching her efforts with the poker.

My experience of lighting many fires during Boy Scout Camps led me to the certainty that this particular fire had no intention of staying alight. 'I don't think you're going to have much luck in keeping that fire alive,' I said.

'Nonsense,' she replied, or words to that effect, 'I'll soon get it going.'

'Would you care to make a bet on that?'

'Alright,' she replied, 'I'll bet you a packet of cigarettes.' The fire quietly died.

Some time later, the day was still young, she approached and presented me with a packet of Players.

'I always pay my debts,' she said.

Somehow, I don't remember how, we found ourselves walking together along O'Connell Street, a long and beautiful street indeed; we passed the famous Post Office and continued towards O'Connell's bridge and the Liffey. For reasons unknown to me, she refused to enter my chosen coffee shop.

I gathered later that this coffee shop was not to her liking. Stupidly, we nearly had a row over it, but she finally entered one of her own choice. Coffee restored our good humour, we chatted on then she said, 'Let me show you my old school,' so we took a tram to the famous Holy Faith, Glasnevin. I cannot remember much about the school but I do recall a quiet walk together around the Glasnevin Cemetery close by, where many of the Irish Patriots lie buried.

Marie, (no longer 'She') pointed out the famous ones as we walked past, nothing morbid about that, rather like a tour around a museum. As we walked along the path our hands bumped together twice, then we were holding hands. It seemed right as we continued our stroll. Thereafter, we saw each other as often as our work would allow. One evening we were saying goodnight in the corridor outside the door of Marie's room, neither of us, it seemed, was anxious for the other to depart. 'Look how late it gets.' Further along, round the bend of the corridor, and out of sight, came loud laughter and footsteps. This would indicate the approach of a group of off-duty male students, under the influence of more than a glass of Guinness imbibed at the local pub. I sensed their mood, they were sure to pass ribald remarks, as they walked past us, remarks that would upset and offend Marie.

Saying, 'You mustn't be caught out here!' in one movement, I had the door open, swung Marie inside, and closed it smartly, just in time as the pleasantly inebriated group thumped around the corner. I advanced boldly towards them on my way to my room.

On district, my last delivery was one of twins. The Mother-to-be had two children already and her antenatal examinations were all normal. She had expressed a wish to continue to have her delivery at home. Everything went smoothly, first one, then the other twin, followed by the after births. Routine follow-up examinations were performed by me but I would not have completed the full number, before my time ran out at the Rotunda and I would need to return to Edinburgh.

I asked Marie if she would deputise for me, we arrived together at their home next day, to introduce her to the family.

Before leaving we were each presented with a glass of sherry and biscuits by the husband as a 'Thank-You'. This put Marie on the spot. She had never taken alcohol yet she did not wish to offend. (Young ladies of Marie's generation, and station were usually teetotal.) I caught her eye, she read my thoughts, accepted the glass of sherry and pretended to sip. She then placed the glass next to mine on the table. It was easy for me to sip from alternate glasses whilst Marie distracted our host.

Killiney Hill

Dawned our last day together, Marie suggested that we visit Killiney, a town a few miles out of Dublin. We could then climb the hill and enjoy the lovely view. We reached the summit after a steep walk and looked around us. A pyramidal shaped structure crowned the hill and on its solid oak door were some hundreds of initials. We added ours, using my trusty penknife. The view was breathtaking and the day was kind, sunshine with just a hint of a breeze. We sat together, hand in hand on the green slopes overlooking Killiney Bay. Silent in our thoughts, we said our 'goodbyes'. The Bard stated well, 'Parting is such sweet sorrow'. The return trip to Scotland on the Irish Ferry was uneventful. I walked the deck with a heavy heart, joining in spirit the thousands of others whom the war had separated, and was now to separate us.

Marie and I were not to know that some years and thousands of miles later we were to meet again, fall in love again, and be married.

Once again the Bard was so right:

'There is a divinity that shapes our ends'.

On arrival in Scotland I lost no time in sending a telegram to Marie.

It read simply:

'Arrived safely.
Love, Leslie.'

CHAPTER SIX

Edinburgh (1941–42)

Fourth Year – continued

BACK TO WORK AGAIN, but now study wise, the academic side was largely under control and I could turn my attention to a major coming event the 'Intervarsities' Boxing Championships'. This year Edinburgh was the host city. We, the members of the boxing club, had obtained permission from the Union Committee to use the Debating Hall for the occasion. A raised boxing ring was constructed and set up on the Palais floor, chairs hired to surround it and the existing galleries would seat dozens more. The high ceilings and numerous large windows would allow adequate ventilation for the event.

At this stage I had reached a peak in my boxing career, very fit and likely to put up a good show on my home ground. The Universities taking part were Edinburgh, Glasgow, Aberdeen and St. Andrews. Alas! A week or so prior to this important event I was struck down by a severe attack of chicken pox, having somehow escaped this infection in my childhood days. Doing nothing by halves, it was a 'LULU'! It produced three sets of crops spread over a week, high fever and prostration. I missed the entire event.

This was, and to some extent still is, one of my life's major disappointments. Some consolation was that our show was a major success with a full house and a high standard of boxing.

The summer term now arrived and with it a resumption of athletic life, at our extensive and lovely sports ground at Craiglochart, some 2 miles from the main University centre. Many a training session and runs I had there. I was a member of the Sports team, representing the University at pole vault. I won the pole vault event that year, and also passed my fourth year in Medicine.

Fifth Year

A twelve month run-up to clear the final bar of medicine, surgery, midwifery, gynaecology, and the clinical bedside examinations at the Royal Infirmary.

Arrangements had been made for final year medical students who were so interested, to live in for an academic term at the Western General Hospital. Together with some ten other students I packed my bag and text books and moved into the hospital hostel, sharing a room with 'John R', one of my friends. The hostel was a two storey stone building, very old, but situated in a quiet area conducive to study. The quarters were comfortable.

Our clinical duties were varied; writing up case notes, admitting new patients, performing routine urine and blood tests, etc. We were free to attend lectures and other essential functions at the Medical School and at the Royal.

As a student group we got on well, all studying for their respective exams, all working hard and no wild parties permitted. I put in an amazing amount of study and revision during those three months at the Western General Hospital, a most satisfying term. Shortly after one of my friends asked me whether I would like to undertake a short spell at the local 'T.B.' Hospital. He had just completed three months there and was about to leave, the post then falling vacant. I sent in my application, attended for interview and was accepted. The post was normally one for post-graduates but the exigencies of war leading to a shortage of available doctors had led to acceptance of final year students as Assistant Medical Officers performing full medical duties.

This was the first occasion that I was offered a salary for my work in hospital, a novel experience!

The hospital buildings were old, solid and grim in appearance. The quarters were comfortable and centrally heated. I was placed in charge of two large wards, one male and one female, whose patients sadly were mostly in advanced stages of consumption. They presented clinically with troublesome cough, some with hectic temperatures, lung cavities, and many whose sputum was positive to bacilli of tuberculosis.

My main duty consisted of ward rounds with a most experienced nursing sister. We had a cheery word for each patient, reviewed their medication, especially their cough sedatives and night sleepers, also wrote up requests for ongoing X-rays of chests, etc. In addition I was on call at night for emergencies occurring in my wards. A senior doctor was in overall charge and available for advice and help if required. There were four doctors at this time and we dined together in an old-fashioned, warm dining room. Leading from the main wards was a small side room which served as a laboratory for various tests, sputum and urine mainly. Patients' sputa were tested monthly for A.F.B. – T.B. Bacillus.

After a few weeks I became expert at preparing the slides, staining them with Ziel Neilson stain heating, then examining them, counting and recording the numbers of A.F.B. per microscopic field.

The sisters and nurses were superb, not only in basic sound nursing of bed patients but in helping to keep up their morale when in fact things were hopeless. I began to dread these night calls, one could do so little, usually to certify a patient's death during the night or witness a massive haemoptysis, as a patient coughed up his/her life's blood.

There was no Streptomycin nor other effective antibiotic in those days. Complete bed rest, high protein nourishing diet and hope were our only weapons against this ancient, remorseless enemy of mankind. It may be of interest to note that Egyptian mummies showed evidence of tuberculosis, over 4,000 years ago. A less depressive duty was to assist the Chest Physician at his Out-patient Clinic where patients with suspected or early tuberculosis were sent for examination, diagnosis and treatment.

The patients' chests were examined with stethoscope and fluoroscope, sputum and blood tests were performed. The Chest Physician was generous in his teaching, allowing me to participate in the examinations, explaining the pathology of what I had seen and heard. He also taught me how to perform a pneumothorax, a simple procedure of collapsing the affected lung by introducing air into the pleural cavity, thereby resting the lung by collapsing it.

During the last few weeks at the hospital, I caught the prevailing 'flu and spent several days in bed. I was coughing fairly strongly, feeling listless and fatigued, common features of early tuberculosis. At the next Out-patient session, I said to the Chest Physician, 'Sir, I think I may have contracted tuberculosis.' He looked at me with gentle eye, 'You're the fourth this week. Shirt off and let's have a look.' Following physical and X-ray examination, he said, 'You're clear, young man. Most medical students go through this worry, at some stage of their course.' What a relief!

The Mackay ménage had now shrunk to two members, Gordon having joined the R.A.F. in medical capacity, with rank of Flying Officer.

Studies for my Finals continued in earnest, right up to the time of the exams, but for a slight hiccup. This came about as follows:

I had promised myself that I would not attend any boxing sessions in my Final Year although keeping up my twice weekly half-hour sessions at the Pollock Gym. However, with the Scottish Intervarsities Boxing Championship due shortly no harm in dropping in to see how the boys were getting on, surely no harm at all! Greeted like a long lost brother I stayed to watch the boys sparring, it was clear to me that we did not have a very strong team. 'Come on, man, change and put on the gloves,' cried Paddy our trainer. I found myself in the ring sparring with the lightweight selected for the coming event to be held at Glasgow that year.

My sparring partner did not like the unexpected competition and turned on the heat. A right hook struck me over the left eye, and I experienced my first black-eye. That really stirred things up, three rounds later I felt that I had held my own.

'Enough,' cried Paddy, 'Come over here lads.' He then made a constructive suggestion that my opponent, several pounds lighter than I, should shed a couple of pounds, enter at the lower division and I take his place.

'You'll be a sure thing at the lower weight,' said Paddy. And so it was, he reached the finals, won, and was later awarded a Boxing Blue.

For myself, not in peak condition, I reached the boxing finals only to lose on points and had to be content with being the runner-up. You can't win them all!

Back to studies, hard work in readiness for the Finals, written, oral and clinical exams, a marathon week of them. Like most students, except perhaps for a small Honours group, I had long dreaded the approach of the Finals. One could pass written and clinicals, only to be failed in the Orals, or indeed any combination of them. All had to be passed.

These thoughts and fears were shared by most of my fellow students. Yet, when the time came, the exams did not prove so formidable. I put this down to solid months of study together with useful experience gained in my undergraduate hospital ward work, a good apprenticeship indeed.

I passed 'M.B.CH.B.' (Edin.) 1942.

With a well earned holiday now possible, Auntie Aggie, Cousin May and I rented a holiday apartment at North Berwick. I un-wound and relaxed in walks along the beach and in playing rounds of golf on that lovely course. How wonderful to feel free! The

My Graduation

My Wife's Graduation

fortnight passed all too quickly, it was now time to arrange my start as a *real* doctor.

But first a letter to Marie in far off Dublin, letting her know that I had passed and enclosing a photo in gown. Back came her reply, 'I have passed too,' and enclosing her photo in gown. We were happy for each other.

During my last term, prior to the finals, I had made contact with the Royal Infirmary at Stirling regarding a post as House-Surgeon. I had been called for interview and had been quizzed by the two senior Surgeons. They were having their mid-morning break from operating and the interview was conducted amicably over a cup of tea, a far cry from the Orals of the Finals. Their questions were wide ranging and not confined to matters surgical. One question related to the life cycle of the Malarial Plasmodium. I gathered that my answers were to their satisfaction. I was later officially informed that I had been accepted for the post.

CHAPTER SEVEN

Stirling (1942–43)

Stirling Royal Infirmary

STIRLING IS A FAMOUS SCOTTISH CITY on the upper reaches of the Forth, within an hour's drive of the Trossachs. It has a long and interesting history and was to be my working-home for the next six months. The S.R.I. in 1942, was a two storey general hospital of some 150 beds, medical, surgical and obstetrical. The consultants of these specialties were highly qualified, all of them Honoraries, being paid only a small stipend, to cover their travelling expenses.

Prior to the formation of the N.H.S. they earned their living in general practice and donated valuable time to the hospital. The resident medical staff consisted of two house surgeons (R.S.O.s), and two house physicians, (R.M.O.s). Apart from our own ward duties we assisted Visiting Honoraries in their Out-patient sessions, in eyes, skins, ear, nose and throat, etc.

We worked hard and long hours, our only time off being a half day a week and one weekend per month.

Emergencies

My surgical colleague and I were on call for 24 hours on alternate days for all surgical emergencies. For minor conditions, should operation be required, the R.S.O. not on call was required to administer the anaesthetic while the R.S.O. on call operated, usually in the Out-patient's theatre. At this time (1942) there was no resident anaesthetist on the staff.

Major Emergencies

For these the R.S.O. concerned would call in his Consultant-Surgeon and also the Honorary anaesthetist, notify the Theatre Sister on duty and have all relevant clinical notes, X-ray films, etc. ready. Finally the R.S.O. would assist at the operation, accompany the patient back to the ward post-operatively, and liaise with the Nursing staff on duty regarding treatment, etc.

The Surgeons

I was fortunate in my surgeons, my chiefs, Dr Angus and Dr Mackelvie were likeable, hard working and rapidly earned my respect.

Dr Angus was a veteran of World War I, having been awarded the O.B.E. and the Military Cross. He was a sound general surgeon with a wide experience.

Dr Mackelvie was younger, with colossal energy, a dynamo, with major interest in urology, and gastric surgery. He performed much research in these fields and later was awarded an O.B.E. for this work.

Both my chiefs were excellent to work with, supportive and appreciative, and expecting a high, all round standard from their R.S.O.s. With the excellent relaxation and anaesthesia obtained by the use of spinal anaesthetics, much of the urological investigations, such as retrograde pyelograms and operative procedures, were thus performed. This was combined with the use of intravenous sedation. Dr Mackelvie was expert at these procedures and after some weeks of watching and learning I was allowed, under strict supervision, to carry out spinal anaesthetics. Much later this was to stand me in good stead.

In this era of 1942, urology was in its infancy. Over the next two decades Dr Mackelvie built up and improved this essential speciality to everyone's benefit in this region of Scotland.

Routine Operating Days

Each surgeon had his own operating day for non-urgent surgical cases, taken from the waiting list. The operation began sharp at 08.00 hours and often extended into the later afternoon. Our mid-morning quarter hour break for tea and biscuits kept us going, and our blood sugar from falling. It also allowed a few minutes for talking shop, and proved a valuable means of communication. Today specialisation would appear to have gone wild, and a general surgeon, or general physician a rarity.

In those days, general surgeons successfully undertook a great variety of surgical conditions, which helped to widen the experience of the assisting staff. It also meant that patients were not shuttled from one subspeciality to another whilst seeking a final diagnosis.

Ward Rounds

I was responsible for two large wards, male and female, of some 20 beds each. In nursing charge were Sister Abernethy and Sister McMillan, the former being much senior and in overall charge. She gave me much useful practical nursing advice. I valued her experience and support. We did ward rounds together at regular intervals, she always had a quiet, cheery word for the patients. Once a week, we also had a major ward round with the surgeons, a separate day for each, and everything had to be right!

Admission of Patients for Operation

Patients admitted from the hospital's waiting list were ushered into the ward, their clothes and belongings recorded and safely stowed away. They were given a warm bath, pyjamas or nightgown issued, tucked into bed and offered a cup of tea. Funny how tea seems to ease any crisis situation. Now came my turn, the patients were given a full medical examination, blood and urine tests performed and a full record of these findings entered on his/her clinical charts. Pre-operative medication and sedation for the night were prescribed and last, but not least, reassurance given to both patient and anxious relatives as to what was to happen on the morrow.

Out-Patient Clinics

Each consultant took his weekly out-patient clinic accompanied by his R.S.O. or R.M.O., to see patients referred by their general practitioner. The R.S.O. kept clinical records, obtained patients' previous X-rays, and other tests, and generally lightened the workload of his/her Chief. All the while the R.S.O. was learning as well as helping, a sound apprenticeship for the future.

Casualty

Much of this work has been described already under the title of 'Emergencies', but here was the first contact with the patient, brought in by car or by ambulance and requiring an accurate diagnosis – acute or non-acute condition?

Complaining of:

1. Lower abdominal pain or discomfort –

    appendicitis, cystitis, etc.

2. Upper abdominal discomfort or pain –

    Peptic Ulcer – acute?

    Peptic Ulcer – about to perforate?

    Acute Volvulus? etc.

Just a few of the many possibilities one has to consider and eliminate. If still in doubt following full examination, the patient was admitted overnight for closer observation. If found non-acute, the patient was allowed to return home to the care of his/her family and the ongoing supervision of his G.P. Altogether an anxious time for an R.S.O. of 24 years of age.

My Colleagues

So far no mention has been made of my three colleagues at the S.R.I. They were Drs Jack, Moyes and Clark, otherwise Bill, Edgar and Logan to each other.

We worked well together as a team, enjoyed each other's company at meals and in our Mess (sitting-room), and the many 'leg-pullings' that went on to keep us sane.

Sadly, over the years, we have lost touch with each other, and are probably scattered far and wide. Our quarters were spartan but comfortable, and centrally heated – a boon when called out at odd hours during a bitter winter's night. We also had a sitting-room and dining-room in our Mess.

During the first few weeks at the S.R.I. fit and full of energy after my fortnight's holiday, I found myself doing hand-stands, using the sides of the old fashioned bath (a solid structure), as parallel bars.

At the end of my six months' term, I could barely raise the energy to slide into the bath, the long hours of work had taken their toll!

It might interest the readers to note that the present compliment of resident Doctors at the S.R.I. I understand, is at least three to four times that of 1942.

Night Rounds

The S.R.I. night nursing routine was in line with the other hospitals in the region. A Senior Night Sister was in overall charge, making several ward visits to each ward during the night. She checked the written reports of the Night Nurses, she was available for nursing advice and often entered a ward to examine a patient, critically ill, at the request of the nurse on duty. The nurses on night duty rapidly developed a sensitive and discerning ear to the footsteps of the Night Supervisor, thus anticipating her arrival.

This gave them time to tidy their desks, have ready their reports, and time to 'make disappear' any extraneous reading matter!

In addition to these nursing measures, the On-Call R.S.O. or R.M.O. was expected to make one such round before retiring. (I won't say for the night, since there was seldom any guarantee of that.) If the wards were quiet, this would take about half an hour, much longer if intravenous drips had to be adjusted or replaced, or other procedures monitored.

Sometimes, when things were quiet and her patients all asleep, the Night Nurse might offer the duty R.S.O. a cup of coffee or tea. The Nurses were allowed to make themselves such cups during their long night shifts, but were not encouraged to share them! If one accepted her offer, and I don't recall any R.S.O. saying 'No', a few pleasant minutes were passed in harmless chatting, with ear ever alerted to approaching footsteps of the Night Super. Then onwards to complete the night round, to fall into bed and hope there would be no urgent calls.

End of Term

Towards the end of my term at Stirling Royal Infirmary I used my weekend leave of the month to visit my Aunt Aggie in Edinburgh, taking the train from Stirling, crossing the Firth of Forth via the imposing Forth Bridge whose railway tracks stood some 150 feet above the water, one admired the view, east and west. Arriving at Waverley Station, then up the windswept stairs to Princes Street, there to catch a tram to Marchmont and home. Both Aunt Aggie and Cousin May were in good health. We passed a pleasant weekend together, giving and getting news of the remainder of the family. Cousin Gordon and Ian were overseas in the Armed Forces, Doreen in government civil administration in Tanganyika, East Africa. Gordon, in the R.A.F. for the past two years, was in the Western Desert of North Africa, his Squadron supporting the 8th Army under General Montgomery. Ian, in the

Army, was now in the Arakan in Burma, in combat with the Japanese Forces.

It would soon be my turn, as the 'baby' of the family, or as Gordon put it later, 'tail-end Charlie'. This is R.A.F. reference to the tail-gunner on Lancaster and Halifax bombers – a highly vulnerable, and dangerous position!

April 1942

My call-up papers arrived informing me to report to the Army School of Hygiene at Keogh Barracks in 4 weeks' time. Logan my R.S.O. colleague was daily expecting his call-up papers and with mine already arrived we felt a farewell party was due.

By good fortune, Bill, who was awaiting his call-up for the Navy, was available and willing to stand-in on duty for the two of us.

Free for the evening, Logan and I, accompanied by two of the nicest nurses of the S.R.I., made a foursome to dine and dance at the local hotel. We had a lovely time, made more poignant by our pending departure, and also that this was the only occasion in 6 months that we four had been able to be off duty together. The next four weeks were busy, tidying up my clinical notes, getting fitted for Army uniform, selecting text books to take with me and many other things. I bade a sad farewell to the S.R.I.

CHAPTER EIGHT

Army Call-Up

Arrival at Keogh Barracks
April 1943

A FAR CRY FROM THE O.T.C., no nonsense here, doctor or no doctor, Army rules and discipline prevailed. We paraded each morning at 08.00 hours, chilly in April, under the charge of a Regimental Drill Sergeant. We marched, we drilled, tried to stand properly at ease and at attention, learned how to give eyes right, to salute, etc.

Not too bad for me, I had experience of this already, but some of the Medicos, now in uniform for the first time, seemed to find it far from easy.

Drill sergeant to his Squad:

'Wake up there!'

'Chest out, back straight.'

'Smarten up.'

'Swing your arms.'

Also, to some individual members, 'Do you have two left feet, sir?'

As Commissioned Officers, (Lieutenant), we out-ranked our Drill Sergeant. *He* was in charge on the Parade ground, softening his often hard criticism by ending it with, 'Sir'.

Towards the month's end, as a Squad, we showed marked improvement, beginning to take pride in our about turns, moving to the right, halting with crisp thud of heavy boots, etc. We forgave our Drill Sergeant for his earlier remarks, what an awkward squad we must have been!! What a headache for him!!

The Army School of Hygiene

Following our daily hour of drill on the parade ground we trooped in for breakfast. A good solid meal considering wartime rationing, and were we hungry! Then to the Army School of Hygiene for lectures and demonstrations in the various aspects of Army life. For example:

1. How to take a sick parade and to deal with the numerous Army forms and procedures.

2. How to use the Horrock's Box to test the acidity and chlorine levels of our drinking water.

3. How to calculate the number of trench latrines per company of men when in the field.

4. How to prevent, as far as possible, the many infections contracted by soldiers in the field or in action, dysentery, malaria, scrub typhus, etc.

5. How a Field Ambulance Unit is organised to treat and evacuate casualties in war time.
    First the A.D.S. – Advanced Dressing Station
    Then the M.D.S. – Main Dressing Station
    The C.C.S. – Casualty Clearing Station
    The A.S.U. – Advanced Surgical Unit.

And so on, each day, teaching us many things, some of which were totally unknown to us.

Amongst those called up with me were several of my University Colleagues in the Class of '42. One of them, William (Bill) approached me saying he was getting married in a week's time, to his fiancée in the V.A.D.s, and would I be his best man. Our batman, or rather our batwoman, a lass from the W.R.A.C.s attached to our Unit, 'Batted' for several Officers, keeping them properly turned out, brass and leather shining, shoes polished, shirt ironed, etc. She entered into the spirit of the occasion, and made sure that Bill and I were superbly turned out on the wedding day. We didn't forget to bring her back a large slice of the wedding cake. It was a quiet wedding, Bill and Anne had a short honeymoon before his being posted elsewhere and finally to the campaign in Italy.

Some months later I learned that Bill, whilst tending his wounded, was killed by shell fire. I wrote to Anne, but what can one say? Sadly many wartime marriages were fated to end this way. Kismet.

101 Anti-Tank Regiment. R.A.

Following my month's training at Keogh Barracks and the Army School of Hygiene, I was posted as R.M.O. (Regimental Medical Officer) to 101 Anti-Tank Regt., stationed at Leigh-on-Sea.

The civilian population on this coastal strip had been evacuated in anticipation of a Germany landing, we were billeted in their quarters. The officers and men were a good bunch and I enjoyed my stay with them, short as it was.

The medical side of my daily routine was not heavy, taking sick parades, inspecting kitchens and quarters, together with regular health inspections of the men in small groups at a time.

From the beginning I believed that one could not adequately fulfil the task of R.M.O. unless one was familiar with the duties, trials and tribulations of the officers and men of the unit. It would do no good, at sick parade to recommend light duties when the soldier or gunner concerned had to lift and carry shells or mortar base plate weighing some 50 lbs. Learning of their various duties took a little time, requiring frequent visits to the various sections, watching them at their duties, asking questions of the N.C.O.s.

The Regiment was equipped with 6-pounder anti-tank guns, mobile and highly efficient. They fired a six pound armour-piercing shell, at very high velocity, with a flat trajectory, a formidable weapon for tanks to face. Regular firing practice was carried out, firing seaward at long range floating targets. As a supernumerary I took my turn, aided by the expert advice of the gun-team. Soon, with the aid of its excellent telescopic sight, I was able to hit the floating targets at 1,000 yard range.

What a gun!! The water boiled where the shell landed, and kept boiling as it churned away its deadly energy. Now to matters more domestic. During a routine inspection of the kitchens, I came across a hanging side of beef, some 150lbs in weight. It was blood stained, the day hot and the meat emitted a strong odour. It was also to be the men's evening meal. At the Army School of Hygiene, we had been instructed to inspect the food in its preparation and, where necessary, to condemn it as 'Unfit for Consumption'. There was no doubt of its strong, unpleasant odour, and its revolting bloodstained appearance. I finally stated 'Unfit for Consumption' and as a result, the men were reduced to a meal of stewed bully-beef that evening!! Later, I heard that a vigorous hosing down and scraping of the surface would have rendered this 150lbs of good beef definitely fit for consumption. The cooks and the men forgave me in the course of time!

Another lesson learned the hard way. As 'R.M.O.' to the 101 A/T Regt. I was responsible to and under the orders of two Commanding Officers:

(1)   The C.O. of the 101 A/T Regt. for all regimental matters and medical matters directly affecting the Unit.

(2)   The A.D.M.S. (Assistant Director of Medical Services) for general medical matters, general instructions, for advice from time to time and also postings.

I paid the A.D.M.S. a courtesy visit to discuss some routine medical matter. I found him approachable and understanding and ventured to raise a personal request. Would the A.D.M.S. arrange an overseas posting for me, as a volunteer for service in the Burma theatre of war?

I explained to him that my parents were in Bombay and that I had not seen them for over 5 years. This was my only chance of meeting them in the foreseeable future. My request was well received, he said he would 'start the ball rolling', but it might take a little time. I departed feeling that he meant what he said and so it turned out.

CHAPTER NINE

Convoy to India

A FEW WEEKS LATER I received orders to report to No. XI depot and Training Establishment, R.A.M.C., to await posting overseas. I cannot recall much of this period other than finding myself on board a large passenger ship in company of some 200 officers and over 5,000 men in a convoy of some 20 ships, guarded by destroyers and frigates. We were 12 to a cabin, normally a four berth, with bunks set in three layers. Lots were drawn when no one, except myself, volunteered for the top bunks, some 6 feet above the floor of the cabin. The early risers became the first shift for shave and wash at the single washbasin, followed by the middle and final shifts. This, after the initial hopeless chaos of 12 men trying to find room to wash, shave and get dressed in such limited space. Nevertheless, all had to be ready and properly turned out in time for breakfast or do without.

The men fared worse than the officers, packed like sardines between decks (A) to (D), in human layers. This was not so bad during the earlier cold, windswept part of the journey, and later round the Cape of Good Hope, but became a major problem during the tropical heat of the final stages of the voyage.

The Mediterranean at this time was a dangerous sea for ships of any description, especially overloaded troop ships. Stuka dive bombers and torpedo bombers of the Jerries dominated this area, operating from bases close to their objectives. The long haul round the Cape was forced on us, the convoy stopping only at Freetown, in West Africa, and Durban in South Africa.

Freetown

Freetown – hot and sticky, nobody allowed ashore, our ships anchored half a mile off the coast. Water, fruit, vegetables etc., were stowed aboard from tenders which came alongside in dozens. In 48 hours the convoy was at sea again. As we neared the Cape it was getting progressively colder, their winter down under. Rounding the Cape our bows pointed northward towards the Equator and warmer clime.

Of interest perhaps, we were following in the wake of the clippers and windjammers of the eighties, ships in which my Father served as a Junior Officer.

Durban

What a relief to be allowed a few hours of shore leave, the local hospitality was overwhelming. South African families met us at the various quays, ushered us into their cars and took us to their homes for meals and drinks. They were keen to hear news of Britain and how the folk were faring. We did our best to oblige.

We found that Cape brandy and ginger ale went well as a long drink and over the next few hours consumed more than we realised. Our ship wasn't dry but had strictly limited bar hours, the obstruction encountered by at least five rows of thirsty officers, ensured that a drink wasn't worth the trouble. Our orders were to report back to the ship by 23.00 hours. So there we were with only seconds to spare, up the gangway, saluted the duty officer at its head, found our cabin and collectively passed out.

Within a day or two the convoy was again on its way, heading northwards into warmer weather. At about latitude 10, at a rough guess, half the convoy steamed to port and the other half to starboard. Was I being taken to the Middle East instead of South East Asia? A quick look at the sun's position reassured me, we were heading north-east for India.

CHAPTER TEN

Homecoming

OUR CONVOY NOW IN THE ARABIAN SEA off the West Coast of India was fast approaching the final run of the course followed by vessels of the British–India Line, which plied during the early part of this century. These ships steamed the round trip to India, passing through the Straits of Gibraltar, the Med, Red and Arabian Seas, to a safe anchorage at Bombay. Their passengers including high officials past and present, Army personnel and their wives and children, essential official correspondence and personal mail. Many years earlier among the B.I. Ships' Officers had been my Father, who had seconded from sail to steam, following the replacement of sail by steam ships. Steaming a few more days, we sighted the *Lady Wilson* Pilot Vessel at anchor in Bombay Harbour awaiting the arrival of all large ships. She had aboard the pilots on duty, who crossed over to the leading ships by motor-boat, hazardous in rough weather, but smooth today.

My Father well remembered the *Lady Wilson* and the many ships he had piloted in all weathers to a safe anchorage. I remember my Father saying that whilst Bombay Harbour was beautiful, it was treacherous, with hidden shoals and rocks, not a perfect harbour like Sydney. I confess to being more than a little excited, nearing familiar places and anticipating meeting my parents again. Security measures were strict, no messages, so my parents had no idea that I was now so close to them. We docked in the late afternoon and no disembarking was permitted until arrangements had been finalised for the morrow. This presented a multitude of problems for the Admin. staff: which unit was proceeding where, and when, and with whom?

In the interval I managed to obtain a leave pass for several hours, caught a taxi and arrived at my parents' palatial apartment at about 07.00 hours, to find them partaking chota hazri (breakfast) on their verandah. I shall not try to describe the emotional side of our meeting only that Dad said, 'You're looking well, son, glad to see you again.' Mother said, 'I knew that Leslie was aboard that convoy, didn't I Chris?' turning to Dad for confirmation. Apparently this was so, Mother had watched the convoy approaching and felt sure that I was aboard. As night fell she became increasingly worried at my non-appearance, aren't mothers wonderful!

We had a pleasant breakfast together, catching up on our family news. Breakfast over, the Indian butler came to remove the breakfast dishes and requested Dad's permission for the staff to meet and welcome the Chota Sahib, the son of the house, me. I found them all lined up in order of seniority, butler, cook, driver, Hamal, and ayah. We greeted each other with old world courtesy. I was both touched and impressed. Soon after, I took off at high speed to see the officer in charge of personnel, and obtained an interview. I poured out my story and was granted 14 days disembarkation – compassionate leave, then to report back smartly for onward posting! Hooray!! A further quick dash to rescue my kit, and back home and a fortnight's reunion with Mum and Dad.

CHAPTER ELEVEN

Posting in India

Field Training

MY LEAVE AT AN END, I was posted as a Medical Officer to General Military Hospital at Dehra Dun, some 800 miles north of Bombay and almost at the foot of the Himalayas. Luckily the season was at its kindest, the tent comfortable, and I had a retired Gurkha soldier as my batman. He saw to my daily needs and obtained for me a genuine Gurkha Kukri, (heavy curved knife) which I carried throughout the campaign. The G.M.H. was running a crash course in medical and related subjects liable to be encountered during service in South East Asia. Useful advice on how best to deal with them was given. There were some six other Officers attending the course and over a few weeks we learned a lot.

Time now for my next posting, which was to 5th Brigade of 2nd British Division, stationed at Ahmadnegar, some 200 miles east of Bombay.

On arrival I found I was to be attached to the 5th Field Ambulance. I reported to the Commanding Officer, Lieut. Colonel J.B. Bunting, and was later introduced to my fellow Officers. The whole of the Field Ambulance was under canvas, the tents pitched on rising ground and well sited.

I was allocated a section of F. Ambulance comprising Sergeant Faulds, Corporal Webb and 18 men, with whom I was to work and command for the next few months in training. We were later to go into action together as a team. The structure of a Field

Ambulance comprised a Headquarter Company and three Sections, R.A.S.C. transport, ambulances, etc.

In action, one section was allocated to each of our three battalions in the 5th Brigade, namely the Camerons, Dorsets, and the Worcesters. The arrangement was flexible, any combination as the situation required. In manoeuvres, of which there were many, each section trained with its parent battalion, and a close liaison was forged. My section was attached to the Worcesters. Individual Section training went on daily, with little let-up.

Reveille began the day at dawn, a quick cup of hot sweet tea whilst shaving and putting on the dress ordered for the day, shorts or longs, belts, puttees, bush shirt, hat, etc. and then on parade. Breakfast, and later a 5 mile cross-country run for all, except essential personnel, (especially not the cooks).

Our C.O. ran with us each day and anyone below his age (circa 38 years), who failed to beat him to the finishing line had to repeat the run later under the eye of our Sgt. Major.

My physical work-outs had languished at Dehra Dun, resulting in my having to repeat the run on the first two days. After that I incurred no further penalties. The remainder of the day was taken up training in many areas, practising bandaging and splinting, applying the Thomas Splint, the pressure point control of haemorrhage and the like. The most physically tiring was, without a doubt, stretcher bearing exercises, carrying a 150lbs soldier as patient. Level ground was bad enough, but up and down elevations in and out of nullahs (river beds) was exhausting.

From hard experience, I can't think of any physical task more demanding, even carrying a 50lb mortar base plate on one's back would be preferable.

The Japanese disregard of the Geneva Convention regarding the treatment of the wounded was experienced during the earlier campaign in Malaya, and more recently in the Burma Arakan. As a consequence it was decided to train and arm F/Amb. personnel to allow them to protect their wounded comrades and themselves should the need arise. We therefore were given instructions in rifle and Sten gun, and even in correct use of the 36 grenade. We became proficient in all these weapons.

Our training sessions continued at a strenuous pace, we were in excellent physical shape. The 5-mile daily run was no effort now, and carrying a 50lb pack, over undulating country in many exercises, was just part of the day's work.

We were soon to be thankful for this degree of fitness. As Christmas approached the tempo of training eased off and limited local leave became available. My leave being granted, I jumped transport to Bombay and was soon reunited with my parents. Both Mum and Dad were looking well, we had heaps of news to relate to each other.

Mother was a lovely lady in face and nature, slim in build, and looking much younger than her years. As wife of the Deputy Conservator of the Bombay Port Trust she felt a double obligation to help the War Effort. She involved herself in many voluntary war tasks, yet found time to continue her previous visits to the many elderly widows living alone, lonely and often impoverished.

Apart from the many small gifts Mother brought them, she had a natural way with her which cheered their existence for a little while.

We arranged a special night out together, a dinner dance at the Bombay Yacht Club of which they had been members for many years. The Bombay Yacht Club was a magnificent building facing the harbour, with many large rooms and conveniences, cathedral ceilings and a large floor area suitable for dancing. The Indian staff had served there for generations, were impeccably attired in spotless whites, and coloured turbans. The turbans indicated their various ranks within the establishment.

The service was silent, soft footed, and efficient, one's every need was anticipated. On taking out a cigarette, one found a 'bearer' at one's side offering a light. Not offering a match, or a modern lighter – not at all – live charcoal in a small earthenware bowl set in silver casing and handle was the source of lighting. The waiters were quick to catch one's eye, and the mere lifting of a hand just a few inches was sufficient to ensure their approach to take one's order. In all this they showed a quiet dignity and dedication to their various tasks. A true reminder of the 'Old Raj' now fast fading away.

The evening was delightful in every way, my parents with me, together in such a comfortable and magnificent setting. I found my Mother to be an accomplished dancer. I don't suppose many sons have this privilege. All too soon my leave was over and back to Ahmadnagar to begin a new phase of our training.

Jungle training

We were transported, as a Brigade, to the Belgaum Jungle, some 250 miles south of Ahmadnagar to undergo jungle training. My section settled in quickly, chopping bamboo to make bunks for themselves and arranging their ground sheets over their mosquito nets to divert the night dew dripping from the leafy canopy overhead. We underwent many training exercises and became accustomed to the many disturbing jungle sounds at night and even the occasional cobra or krait, two very poisonous snakes. It was interesting some years later to read and compare the account of Spenser Chapman on jungle lore in his book, *The Jungle is Neutral*.

Our section took its turn to wash and bathe in a nearby river, marching along a jungle track, thick with dust, consequent on the long dry season. On our return to camp we were clothed in fine red dust. After several such sessions I decided (unwisely) to try to find an alternative route back to camp via the jungle. I sent on my section under charge of the Corporal, Sergeant Faulds and myself began our trek.

There were three points of reference in an otherwise featureless jungle;

(1)   The dusty track

(2)   The river

(3)   The railway line.

I planned to take the hypotenuse of the triangle so formed in our return to camp. With map and compass we should have been all right. Not so, our passage was constantly barred by closely growing major clumps of bamboo, yards wide, which we had to circumnavigate. This made our compass bearing difficult to follow and forced errors in my calculations.

After some 2 hours we were off-course, hard to estimate how far we had walked and which direction to take. Twilight had already set in, within an hour it would be dark, pitch dark. Was that coughing grunt from that skilled night stalker, the leopard? With only my service revolver for protection! Imagination can run riot in such a tense situation, put a firm curb on it lad!

My guardian angel again to the rescue, a prolonged whistle from our right flank indicated the presence of the elusive railway line – only 100 yards away but totally out of sight. We could otherwise have paralleled the line or worse, deviated from it. In hindsight, I shudder at the possibilities.

We arrived at the camp in darkness to find all members worried and Corporal Webb wondering what action he should be taking. They plied us with sweet hot tea and bully stew, never tasted better! The remainder of our training at Belgaum was uneventful. Back again at Ahmadnagar, to hear rumours of a recreation break for the Division which had been in hard training for months. Too good to be true!!

The Japanese forces launched an attack in strength and speed, with their 15th, 33rd and 31st Divisions. Through Northern Burma they came, aiming at Imphal, Kohima then Dimapur. From there, the gateway to the Eastern Plains of India lay open. Goodbye Leave!! The balloon had gone up.

CHAPTER TWELVE

Action – Kohima

Zubza, Meremer, Naga Village, Imphal, Tamu

The balloon has gone up. Japanese forces invade Assam.

Every unit of the 2nd British Division was activated in a race across India to Assam to assist in halting the enemy advance. 2 Div., the main reserve division, the other already involved mainly in the Imphal and Arakan sphere of operation. India was some 1,200 miles wide, from Bombay to Calcutta, but no adequate direct land route existed across the subcontinent.

A long loop north-east, then one south-east from Allahabad a total of some 1,800 miles by road was necessary to reach Calcutta.

Every form of transport was utilised, air, rail, and road, the infantry mainly by air. I was detailed to take medical charge of one of the many motor convoys crossing India on way to Assam.

24 March 1944

Journey began, my staff and I travelling in and driving ambulances.

Route as follows:
AHMADNAGAR – MHOW – BIORA – SHIVPURA – JHANSI – CAWNPORE – ALLAHABAD – BENARES – DERRA – BAGODA – ASANSOLE – CALCUTTA.

Following 12 days in transit, we arrived at Calcutta. Mepacrine prophylaxis against malaria began, one tablet a day every day. Much needed rest period for 48 hours, including essential maintenance of our vehicles. Officer 1/c Convoy and I took the opportunity to have a good meal at Firpos Restaurant, a real relief from our 'Road-Rail' rations.

8 April 1944

Calcutta. Vehicles loaded onto long, low railway waggons, slept in ambulances, progress slow, many stops and shunting to allow troops' trains priority in their dash to Assam.

11 April 1944

Siliguri reached, vehicles detrained, and parked for the night, following routine maintenance.

Slight Diversion

Hugh and I drove our jeep some 50 miles to Darjeeling, a nearby hill station. Little Himalayan railways crossed the climbing road innumerable times, we had to keep a sharp look out for its little locomotive appearing suddenly in front of us from either flank.

Darjeeling, a pleasant town, set on hillside some 7,000 feet above sea level and therefore cool in climate. Friendly smiling hill people, seemingly happy in their lives greeted us.

Following a short look around and a quick cup of tea and cake we hurried back to camp.

Siliguri 12 April 1944

Convoy set off by road, our route now being; COOCHBEHAR – GAUHATI – NONGONG – GILAGHAUT – DIMAPUR. We crossed the sacred river, the Ganges, at Benares. We had a little adventure at Coochbehar, an Indian State, with its own government and royalty.

Hugh and I taking an evening stroll, walked past the Palace gates, and stopped to talk to the Sentry. Whilst so talking, two Indian ladies in beautiful saris strolled by taking their evening promenade. We saluted and greeted them, it seemed that the elder was one of the Royal Princesses and the younger her lady-in-waiting and most attractive. We saluted once again and continued our stroll.

Dimapur 16 April 1944

The main railhead, and Army depot supplying our troops in the Kohima and Imphal area of operations.

Onward to Zubza, along a narrow twisting road, rising 2,000 ft. with sheer drop over the khud (hillside) on one side, and steep mountain on the other. The Camerons and Worcesters, our two leading Battalions had already made contact with the enemy, encountering a Jap road-block at milestone 32, which took several determined attacks to clear. The initial attack was led by Major Elliott of the Worcesters – First 2 Div.'s encounter with the enemy.

Zubza 17 April 1944 – 2,000'

Now established as firm base for the 5th Brigade, where I joined my parent unit, the 5th Field Ambulance, under the command of Lt/Col. J.B. Bunting. Our Padre, one to each battalion, was Captain (Father) B. Fitzgibbon, posted to us after the tragic death of Revd. Father J. O'Callaghan, killed by enemy action only a week previously. Father Fitzgibbon and I were to share many tight corners together over the next few months.

Barbed wire and slit trenches surrounded the Brigade perimeter but right now a shortage of available combat personnel to man it adequately, everyone was needed. Father Fitzgibbon and I, together with our section of Field Ambulance, manned our sector of the brigade perimeter from dusk to dawn, 2 hours on – 2 hours off, the off person trying to sleep at the bottom of the trench, knees up to chin, sten gun to hand, whilst his companion kept guard, and so on, for the first two nights.

Meanwhile the garrison at Summer House Hill, (also known as

Garrison Hill and Hospital Hill) including the area of the District Commissioner's bungalow and tennis court were holding out against fanatical Japanese attacks. Very fierce fighting, constant night attacks, heavy casualties. From the Zubza area our 25 pounder guns of the Royal Artillery, were now able to give the besieged garrison valuable supporting fire.* The garrison consisting mainly of the 4th Royal West Kents and Assam rifles must be relieved, it would be a close thing.

Our attack launched on 18 April 1944

All three Brigades of 2 Div. as follows:
   5th Brigade – left hook to Meremer Spur
   4th Brigade – right hook via Mount Pulebadze
   6th Brigade – down road to Kohima

5th Brigade commanded by Brigadier Hawkins, D.S.O., M.C.
   Night attack, a left hook towards the hill feature of Meremer, to strike the enemy from the north east.
   Night pitch dark.
   Rain falling.
   Men and mules to carry essential ammunition and food.
   My medical pack weighed 50 lbs., sten gun and ammunition some 10 more pounds, no clear track to follow, slippery under foot, and steep slopes to traverse.
   A halt eventually called to await first glimpse of dawn, to assess our position and obtain our bearings. Our guide was an English speaking educated Naga called Savino. First experience of enemy shell fire, Jap 75mm. shells whizzed overhead, they had not pin-pointed our position, harassing fire only, nobody hurt.
   Dawn: Misty, essential to reach our hill destination before full

---

* Reference reading of the seige at Kohima: *The Siege* by Arthur Campbell, *Kohima* by Arthur Swinson

light, we slogged uphill, made it in good time to get established on the hill feature of Meremer.

Digging of slit trenches began at once, to aid in defensive perimeter and cover from enemy mortar or shelling. This was our pattern throughout, moving from one dominant hill feature to another as the tactical situation demanded – a game of chess with the enemy. Average levels of operation some 3,000–5,000 feet, with ravines in between, down one side and up the other, carrying our heavy packs, exhausting work. We were thankful for our previous intensive training and physical fitness.

Meremer

Second night, one of our three battalions moved to another feature, perimeter had to be tightened. My section and I took over our portion of perimeter. I found myself acting Infantry Platoon Officer, two hours on, two hours off once again. Small Jap patrol spotted searching for our position, night dark and range too far, our fire control excellent, our position not given away.

20 April 1944

On the move again to another dominant peak, closer to Kohima. Rain falling again, men and mules slipping on the wet slopes, very hard going and at a fast pace. Tore the guts out of one, the last 400 yards covered had a gradient of one in three. Heavy Jap opposition encountered, leading battalion had already incurred casualties; coming to their aid further casualties were incurred by our own group. Our Commanding Officer detailed me to take charge of the evacuation of the wounded, forming a large stretcher party, with an infantry platoon from the Worcesters as defensive escort.

No roads in this sector, hence no motor transport.

Evacuation of Casualties to Zubza

Thank heavens the rain had ceased. Our stretcher party and escort

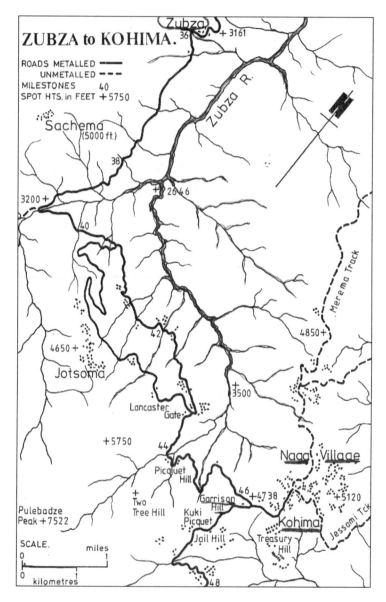

Map reproduced from "March On" by courtesy of author,
Norman Havers, M.B.E.

Three Nagas

moved off to rendezvous with a Naga porter group, coming to meet us from Zubza. The mountain paths were primitive and narrow tracks, beaten by the feet of Nagas walking to and from their villages sited on the hill tops. Our column in single file stretched over 800 yards. Hard work for everyone including myself. I had to move up and down the walking column to attend to the wounded.

At point of rendezvous, I happened to be at the rear of the column and could not sight its van – no walkie-talkies in those days. On arrival at the rendezvous I found that the casualties had been taken over by the Naga porters and were well on their way, including most of the infantry escort. The Nagas had brought with them medical supplies, and spare stretchers and this large pile greeted me. My orders ran out here, and with the remaining W/T set, I tried to make contact without success.

Problem;

(1)   Not now enough men to carry this heavy equipment any great distance.

(2)   Had our 5th Brigade meanwhile moved to another hill feature?

(3)   Where to go from here?

Decided to try and reach Zubza before dark, carrying this equipment back to them. Going heavy and night approaching, had to reach Zubza before dark, many trigger-happy warriors on the perimeter defences at stand-to and thereafter.

Further Decision: No chance of tired men reaching Zubza whilst carrying these heavy loads. Found a suitable cache to hide our medical stores, marked the position on my map and hurried my party onward. The last half mile was uphill and steep, I led the column, and Sgt. Taylor whipped on the tail end. We slogged up that slope, panting and perspiring, many of the men on their last legs, just about had it myself. We entered the brigade perimeter just before dusk and our stand-to.

The cook Sergeant produced bully stew and hot tea for us all, our first meal since an early cold snack 12 hours ago. We must have covered some 12 miles, over terrible terrain, lovely country, but not a yard of it level, carrying heavy packs, and a fair share of the stretcher bearing.

Slept like a log.

Next morning, set out again with a fresh party to rescue our equipment from its overnight cache, thus avoiding the wrath of my Commanding Officer.

Out again, this time with a group of Naga porters to meet further incoming casualties from our brigade. Met them, handed care of casualties over to the Medical Officer of the column, and continued on with my section to rejoin our 5th Brigade, which had indeed moved to another hill feature. Found the Brigade without incident, they were already well dug in, several days in situ followed. Japs on adjacent Fir Hill, also well 'dug-in', each side awaiting the other's move. A frontal attack would be costly of casualties, instead the Brigade would make a night march to by-pass them, and to occupy a further hill position behind them and closer to Kohima.

Surprise was achieved

Naga Village, at 5,000 feet, occupied by our leading troops just before dawn. Main body followed promptly, but rear party encountered Jap sniper and L.M.G. fire, causing sizeable casualties. My section and I attended to the wounded on the spot, but how best to get them back to the M.D.S. (Main Dressing Station) at Zubza? Enlisted the aid of the crews of the Bren carriers; casualties loaded, and with tank escort got them safely away, thank the Lord. Made our way to the Brigade position crowning the hill, every one digging like mad! Before our slit trenches could be fully dug and usable we were subjected to mortar fire from the enemy. I was assisting a wounded soldier, shot through the upper arm, when one of the mortar bombs landed 10 feet away killing three men, including the one I was helping. The jagged fragment must have missed me by inches. Jake, several feet further away, had several dents made in his steel helmet from secondary rock fragments. That night I said a prayer of thanks and a prayer for our dead comrades.

Digging continued, shelters made using tarpaulins, for the wounded. Rain that night, start of the monsoon season. (Early May).

Adjacent hill feature 5120 now occupied by our leading battalion. Japs reacted fiercely, attacked in strength, forcing them to return to Naga Village and regroup. Casualties continued to mount, Naga Village now cut off by Jap reinforcements, the only road blocked, not now possible to evacuate our casualties. Air drop received from DC3 (Dakotas) of variable supplies, food, medicine and ammunition. Several further such drops to us over the next two weeks. Stalwart fellows, these pilots.

First night on Naga village, wet and worrying, with intermittent mortar and 75 mm gun fire from the enemy. Digging continued and tarpaulin shelters improved to keep the rain off our wounded. Hot cups of tea and reassurance to help keep up their spirits during the long night. After a re-check of their dressings and wounds, gave them a further shot of morphine to ease their pain and give them sedation.

Next afternoon – our tanks and infantry had reopened the road skirting the foot of Naga Village, Bren Carriers and armoured ambulance brought in to carry the wounded back to the M.D.S. at Zubza.

Amongst the wounded was Brigadier Hawkins, shot through hand and thigh by a sniper's bullet, fortunately a 'through and through', missing bone and major arteries. One case stands out in my memory, that of a young gunner R.A. Officer, badly wounded by fragment of a mortar bomb and in severe surgical shock. His wounds were dressed, injection of morphine given, and two pints of plasma transfused. He showed much courage and a determination to live, which carried him through. Some weeks later a letter from him reached me. Though still in hospital he was making good progress. Our team felt well rewarded.

Sergeant Faulds and his section, under my charge proved equal to the many tasks they had to perform, doing everything possible, and more, under the most trying conditions. I salute them.

Nagas: A word here about the Nagas, all volunteers from hilltop villages, and a tremendous help in carrying our wounded to safety. Hillmen all, well muscled, four to a stretcher, they made light work of their heavy load. We owe them a great deal, also the District Commissioner Sir Charles Pawsey, M.C. who organised his Nagas throughout the campaign.

Some ten days thus at Naga Village

Rain – heavy, intermittent. Limited shelter for our A.D.S. Casualties mounting. Mortar fire, sniper fire, 75 mm shell fire experienced.

One night particularly bad, our air drop of ammunition had been blown away by strong winds, the parachutes' contents falling into Japanese hands.

That night they fired back our 3 inch mortar bombs, our A.D.S. repeatedly straddled.

Morale good, my men heartened me greatly, their spirits grand, some good jokes, at a critical time, did much to help our situation.

Finally a 75 mm Jap shell, landed a few yards away, put several fragments through our ration packs, a 3 inch mortar bomb exploded right into our slit trenches fortunately unoccupied at the time.

This, after some 10 days of such treatment, forced a move to a nearby nullah, but not all rosy there either. True, less flak flying about, but that nullah seemed to drain half of the hillside, and was it raining!! Deep flood drains were dug and upper slope heavily sandbagged, situation stabilised.

The Main Dressing Station was also functioning, with its greater facilities and better cover for our casualties. This allowed us safer if wetter, temporary abode.

Relief

After over 3 weeks on Naga Village, our 5th Brigade was relieved by 33 Brigade of 5th Indian Division. We returned to our Zubza base on 21 May, for rest and sleep, wash and bath, (courtesy of Mobile Bath Units) change of jungle greens, hot meals.

4 June

Action again, 5th Brigade ferried by motor transport (what luxury!) to Treasury Hill.

A.D.S. set up , the final phase of battle of Kohima now began. Our section of field ambulance worked forward to collect casualties from the attack on Dyer Hill, mainly Dorset casualties. Deep valley intervened, a very hard carry involved. From Treasury Hill, we witnessed two infantry attacks on Jap positions.

Big Tree Hill

Attack carried out by the Camerons, with supporting fire from Vickers Machine guns of the Manchesters and 25 pounders from the R. Artillery.

Pimple attacked from Dyer Hill by the Camerons, supported by 3.7 howitzers, and tank 75 mm guns.

A magnificent view of the barrage and attack, seen from close quarters, fire directed at the Jap bunkers. The Camerons captured the position, sadly losing a well liked officer, killed while leading the attack.

Pfuchama, 4,907 feet, June 5th

For 5th Brigade, and others, objectives here were dominant features, peaks some 4–5,000 feet above sea level from which to operate. Good hard slogging over mountain tracks, always a valley to cross and then reclimb the other side.

Mules, including Old Handle Bars, carried the heaviest equipment, the going so steep in parts that members of the R.E. (Royal Engineers) had to cut steps for them – a slow business at times.

It would seem that the humble mule has a well developed sense of what constitutes a fair day's work.

Too heavy a load for too long builds up resentment in the mule culminating in its throwing off its load. At times many of us wished we could do the same. Pfuchama reached, luckily no enemy encountered, Worcesters continue as the leading battalion, on to Phesema. On our way, slopes very steep, a barbary mule (one overloaded and resentful), threw its whole load over the Kludside (hillside).

Cruel work fetching up the load, scattered in its fall, the mule, poor animal, called some shocking names.

Phesema reached without further resistance, no Japs encountered.

Overall Picture at this Stage

(1)   Road Blocks cleared of Japs to our West.

(2)   4th Brigade – right hook over the massive Aradura Spur completing the pincer movement to join us at M.S. 52.

(3)   6th Brigade including Dorsets, Durhams, Royal West Kents, Royal Berks. Rajputs, Gurkhas and Assam Rifles, had cleared Jap forces from Garrison and surrounding hills, after some of the most bitter fighting of this Campaign.

(4)   Kohima now in Allied hands, mopping up of stray Jap forces continued.

Phase 1 completed.

Phase 2

(1)   The clearing of all Jap forces from the Kohima-Imphal road,

(2)   The opening of the road to supply and to feed our troops (4th. Corp) at Imphal and beyond.

Worcesters still the leading battalion, on to Kegwema at M.S.53., where they joined up with the Royal Berks. coming down from the Aradura Spur.

Kegwema. (M.S.54). The site of previous I.G.H. (Indian General Hospital) with numerous bashas (bamboo huts) providing adequate shelter, sufficient water supply, and access to the road.

Our M.D.S. set up here, soon joined by the A.S.U. (Advanced Surgical Unit). A satisfactory arrangement, allowing good functioning, followed by easy evacuation of casualties. Our forward troops, Worcesters, Camerons, and Dorsets, pushing hard along the Manipur road towards Imphal. Their casualties could now be whisked back to us by road ambulances in a matter of minutes rather than hours. (At last).

At Kegwema the Advanced Surgical Unit operated on our battle casualties, whilst we, at our M.D.S. set up Sick Bay Wards to treat

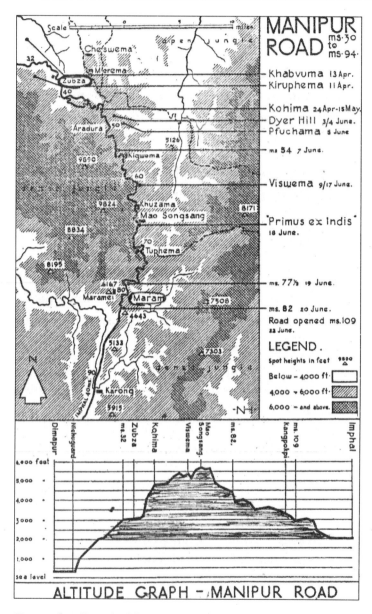

Drawn by Captain Norman Havers, M.B.E.

the many cases of dysentery/diarrhoea, break through malaria, etc., inevitable during any military campaign. I became a physician again and almost a base wallah!

Viswema (M.S.60) Some miles further down the Manipur road was the site of strong Japanese rearguard action, heavy rain falling throughout.

June 17th

Big attack went in, preceded by heavy barrage from Div. artillery, mortars and tank fire.

Worcesters and Camerons led the attack. Japs driven off and positions secured. Our casualties much less than expected.

Mao Songsang (5500) feet M.S.65. The highest point on the Manipur Road, taken after heavy barrage, Japs pulled out.

Onward to Maram Spur (M.S.81). The last organised Jap resistance before Imphal.

June 19th

Fine and clear at last, after 10 days of continuous rain. Worcesters in the lead, searching for Japanese bunker positions, found many of them on Maram Spur.

Attack began with heavy artillery barrage and a creeping type of fire just ahead of forward troops, coloured tracer fire from Bofors guns guided the barrage, together with use of smoke grenades from the leading companies. Position taken, led by Major Tooby and 'B' Company, Major Watson, 'A' Company, and Captain Parton.

June 22nd 1944

At milestone 109, our leading battalion made contact with elements of 5th Indian Div. coming up to meet us from Imphal. The Kohima-Imphal Road was now open, from the railhead at Dimapur through to Imphal.

Phase 2 now completed.

In three months, our 2nd. Division had played a major role in smashing the Jap 31st Div. had advanced some 77 miles, against most bitter opposition. It had assisted, in a major role in smashing the Japs' hopes of an invasion of India.

Our 2nd. Division had also incurred heavy casualties, 1300 killed and three times this number wounded, many of whom may not have survived their injuries.

> When you go home,
> Tell them of us, and say,
> For your tomorrow, we gave our today.

Imphal

A military camp, airstrips, a tented hospital and collection of bashas plus monsoonal rain.

This was to be our divisional camp for a few weeks to allow rest, refit, and rehabilitation.

The 23rd. Indian Division had now taken over 2 Div's role of pursuing the Jap forces down the Imphal-Tamu road, turned into a mud track by the monsoon rain.

Sick Bay set up for the treatment of the many minor and not so minor, medical conditions developed during the Kohima campaign.

The men were encouraged to come for treatment, diarrhoea, dysentery, fevers and skin conditions predominating.

Inoculations needed to be brought up to date, especially those against tetanus, typhoid and paratyphoid. Kept very busy.

A visit from the 'Supremo' Lord Louis Mountbatten livened the scene. He gave a down to earth talk, standing on an ammunition box, surrounded by the officers and men of the Battalion. Lord Louis covered the major achievements to date and the broad strategies to be followed in the immediate future. He also congratulated 2Div. as having performed a magnificent job. It seemed only fair that someone 'High up' should say so.

Within the Forgotten Army (14th. Army), 2Div. seemed more forgotten than most.

Action Again

IMPHAL—PALEL—MOREH—TAMU—LOCKCHAO RIVER
(Through the Kabaw Valley)
5th Brigade 2 Div. now moved down the Imphal-Tamu track, to relieve the 23rd Indian Div. Brigade and to take over pursuit of the retreating Jap forces.

21 July 1944

Battalion embarked and driven to Palel, now an advanced fighter-bomber base, with Squadrons of Hurricanes and 'Hurribombers' continuing to harass the retreating enemy.

Onwards to Malta and Gibraltar, two hill features at M.S.40. Mileage now measured from Imphal.

Slit trenches, surrounded by barbed wire, well sited for defence, crowned their peaks. This was the general area where the Jap forces, advancing on Imphal were halted, in bitter fighting, by the 17th and 20th Indian Divisions, and others too. (N.B. An Indian division consists of three brigades, each of three battalions, two Indian and one British. They worked and fought well together.)

Malta and Gibraltar had been pounded by the Jap 150 mms. 105 m. shells, and still, months later bore signs of this barrage.

Scraggy, yet another defensive position, to the right of the track, showed even more evidence of the pounding it had received. All vegetation and trees had been blasted away. Worcesters and our section of Field Ambulance spent the night in the defensive position of Malta.

Monsoons now showered us with inches of rain, slit trenches filling rapidly with the run off of water.

A Worcester soldier was seen solemnly bailing out his overflowing slit trench with his mess tin!

A pump capable of removing 100 gallons a minute would have made little difference to his situation!

We laughed, and laughed and laughed.

The ground all around and the tracks became a sea of clinging mud. Our mules were a wonderful help in carrying our stores, largely food and ammunition. We carried heavy packs ourselves feeling like human mules at times. As one mule to another, they had our full sympathy!

Hong Kong and Columbo were two further defensive peak positions encountered on our way to Tamu.

Both were used in stubborn defence against the advancing Jap forces, some months earlier.

Bulldozer Ridge our next position for the night, the Japs fast retreating, we had temporarily lost contact.

The Tamu Road. Reproduced by permission of the Imperial War Museum, London.

Vital air supply dropped to us, parachutes for most of the supply, free drop of bales of hay for the mules, 'gardez-vous'!

Pushed on next morning, Worcesters the lead battalion, objective now Tamu and the Lockchao River crossing.

Spur a further defensive position *en route*, slit trenches surrounded by barbed wire on hill top, we occupied this position for the night.

A most unfortunate accident occurred there just before dusk. Someone trod on a concealed trip wire and exploded an anti-personnel mine. Nine Worcesters were injured, two seriously, the others with minor wounds. We attended to their injuries and had them ferried by 4-wheel drive ambulance to our M.D.S. which was following us.

August 4th 1944

Moreh now reached, right on the border of Burma itself, so far we had been fighting on Assam Territory.

Worcester patrols active in forward areas, had now reached the airfield at Tamu.

Tamu. Many Japanese dead lined the road edges, they must have fallen out during the retreat and died where they fell. In every hut and shelter were more dead Japs, others sick and starving, too weak to move, or to commit their traditional hara-kiri. Their line of communication and supply was now non-existent, no supplies, no food, no medicines, no hope. With my Jeep ambulance, we picked up a few Jap soldiers too weak and too sick to resist. Our field ambulance M.D.S. sent up a section to assist in their collection and evacuation to M.D.S. and onwards. A Burmese Temple passed on our way, a quick look inside revealed some dozen Japanese dead.

In the hot, steaming, airless Kabaw Valley, the stench of death lay heavy – well named the Valley of Death. Many of the Japanese dead would be accounted for by the constant strafing and low

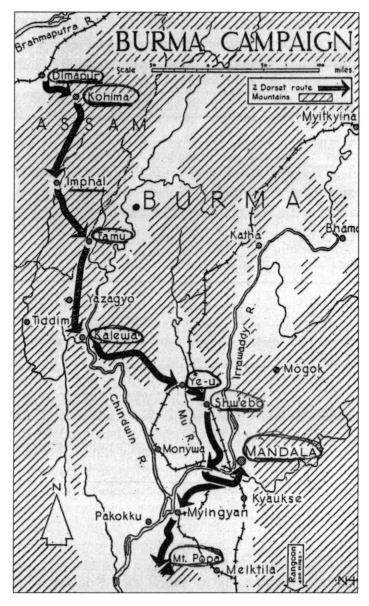

The part of the 2nd Division in the Assam-Burma Campaign.
Map drawn by Captain Norman Havers., M.B.E.

level bombing by our Hurricanes. There is little doubt, however, that the chief causes of death were starvation, and malaria, working together as a grim team.

The Kabaw valley was reputed to be one of the heaviest malarial areas in south east Asia, it certainly lived up to its reputation. Even with sound anti-malarial measures, plus daily Mepacrine tablets, we suffered quite a knock ourselves. Our immediate objective was now achieved, that of clearing Jap forces out of this area, and establishing a bridge-head over the Lockchao River. Our brigade forces (the 5th Brigade) stood firm, and allowed the 11th East African division to pass through us and to take over role of pursuit.

Their objective now was to drive back the Japs, further and finally to establish a bridge-head over the Chindwin River at Kalewa.

A few days later we retraced our steps through the Kabaw Valley to Imphal, and then onward to Maram Spur, the one captured by the Worcesters earlier on. Maram Spur was to be our camp for the next few weeks, for rest, refit, and training of reinforcements.

Photograph taken from Maram Spur 4,000–6,000 feet altitude. (1944.)

CHAPTER THIRTEEN

Maram Spur 4000 feet

Rest, Refit, Retrain
August 12th 1944

THE WORCESTERS ARRIVED AT MARAM SPUR IN THE AFTER-
NOON of the 12th August in pouring rain, hillside dripping
wet, with its access track temporarily impassable to motor transport,
even the four wheel drives.

A depressive sight, general moans all round, nothing for it but
to set up camp for ourselves.

Fortunately many tarpaulins had been captured in the Tamu
area, which greatly helped in the setting up of shelters for the
night and protection from the rain.

Now officially posted as Regimental Medical Officer to the 7th
Battalion, the Worcesters, the work for me began in earnest:

(1)   Camp sanitation – Top priority.

(2)   Setting up of R.A.P. and Sick Bay to treat sickness con-
       tracted by the men, *en route.*

(3)   Inoculations to be brought up to date.

(4)   Examination and assessment of reinforcement personnel
       posted to us from within the Division.

(5)   Many other tasks as they arose.

Monsoon rain now starting to ease, our camp looking shipshape,
good hill site, tents erected, and now in use. Weather improving,
warm sunny days, not too hot at 4000 ft level.

Sick Bay now completed, with a dozen stretcher beds, sited adjacent to our R.A.P.

Most useful to be able to treat the sick on the spot, rest in bed if necessary, with less need for onward evacuation for treatment, and hence sometimes lost to the battalion. As found at Imphal,

Sick Bay. "Maram Spur" 7 Worcester Regiment. Sgt. Middleton and Staff. (August – November 1944)

the main medical conditions requiring treatment were diar-rhoea/dysentery, skin conditions and fever break through of malaria.

Despite strict anti-malarial precautions and daily Mepacrine the mosquitoes of the Kabaw Valley had done their work, inflicting varieties of subtertian malaria, some partially resistant to Mepacrine.

Some of the sick personnel required more intensive treatment at the main dressing station of 5th Field Amb. or at forward hospitals.

Others required surgery for conditions such as hernia developed during the long marches with heavy packs, up and down the Naga Hills. These conditions required examination and assessment, clini-cal recording, filling in related Army forms, and arrangements for their transport, and evacuation.

Tooth abscesses, painful cavities, etc. found in our servicemen, were referred to the Dental Officer, at the Dental Clinic situated at the Main Dressing Station close by and treated locally.

Scrub Typhus – This condition presented an additional health hazard, spread by the bite of a free living mite in grass or scrub. Our first such encounter was in the Kabaw Valley, leading to many cases. On Maram Spur there were patches of hillside infested by these mites, as shown by the occurrence of new cases.

A severe systemic disease with fevers, prostration, often delirium, extreme weakness and a considerable mortality. The Eschar at the site of the bite was a nasty looking dark coloured rounded indurated lesion, once seen never forgotten. Within a few days the patient was desperately ill. Our Field Ambulance set up a special tented hospital, bringing in doctors, nurses, and essential medication, in order to treat those severely ill patients on the spot. A long bumpy ambulance ride, with much handling would decrease their chances of survival. It is interesting to note that Chloramphenicol was one of the few earlier antibiotics to be effective in this condition.

Prevention – A major effort was speedily organised:

(1)   Known areas of infestation by the mite were charted on all maps, and placed off limits.

(2)   Puttees were substituted for gaiters to help seal off entry of the mite an ankle level. Sleeves to be kept rolled down except when on fatigues or in camp.

(4)   D.B.T. – Dibutylphthalate solution to be rubbed on to the puttees and socks, sleeve edges, fore-arms, neck, etc. Daily application to kill the mites.

These measures proved effective, only an occasional case now occurring. Following many weeks of hard work by my staff and myself and ready help provided by the various companies and platoons, the Camp was now in good medical order. Flies were practically eliminated, tented kitchens and work areas clean and functioning well, medical conditions under control, and the latrines almost show places.

I could now relax and take my overdue leave.

About this time I received a letter from my school friend John Morrison. John had volunteered for the Royal Artillery he had been accepted and put through the O.C.T.U. (Officers Training Course).

He emerged from the course with the rank of Lieutenant. On the opening of the second front in Europe, John took part in the early savage actions.

While giving supporting 25 pounder fire to our leading troops, John was struck by a piece of shell fragment from German counter-battery fire.

The fragment pierced his chest, entering his lung, a major injury. He was operated on and evacuated to Britain. He was later demobilised and allowed home to Scotland. Thankfully he made a good recovery.

Leave in Bombay

Accompanying me on leave were Harry Parton and Barney Tar-buck, Officers of the Worcesters.

A hot slow journey to Dimapur, descending from some 4000 ft above sea level at Maram, to some 500 feet over the twisty narrow road. Held up for two days, several landslides blocking the road, following a sudden downpour of 6 inches of rain. Full marks to engineers and their teams, for clearing the road so promptly.

Dimapur – our major base and railhead supply source to our troops. Military Hospital sited there, and treating many of our wounded.

Called to see them and have a chat, their morale excellent. Whom should I bump into in one of the wards, but Sister McMillan, late of Stirling Hospital, now enlisted in the Q.A.s as Nursing Sister, Lieutenant McMillan.

What a coincidence, many theatres of war and so many hospitals! It was good to see her and we exchanged news and shared a long tea session.

Our journey resumed by train to Calcutta – one best forgotten! – followed by a pleasant one to Bombay. Happy reunion with my Father and Mother.

I was glad to find that Dad had recovered from being literally blown-up by the explosion of a munition ship, S.S. *Fort Stikine* which caught fire on 14 April 1944 whilst unloading. As Deputy Conservator he was supervising the operations when the explosion occurred. He was thrown sky high and tossed into the dock, sustaining a compound fracture of the ankle and a perforated eardrum, apart from the surgical shock involved. His Indian driver, Bahgwan, and car, waiting some distance away, were disintegrated by the blast and never found. A quirk of fate indeed, I without injury through the Kohima campaign, yet my Father in Bombay so injured.

Harry, Barney and I proved good companions, spending our

leave together. We had many meals and chats at home with Mum and Dad, recounting some of our adventures. We also had swimming sessions and drinks at the Yacht Club. There we met two Nursing Sisters also on leave, and we formed a pleasant group.

We had almost forgotten what it was like to be in female company!

Our leave ran out all too soon, and the long tedious journey back to Maram Spur began, arriving on 23rd September.

We three resumed our separate duties in the Battalion. There was much to be done over the next few weeks in preparation for our pending action in Burma itself. At the end of the day's work we washed changed and met at our tented mess for supper.

The tent, large with lateral extensions, served as a dining room, lounge and after hours as a bar. It was situated on a slope close to the officers' lines, looking over the Naga Hills, with a vista, extending for miles.

Some devastatingly beautiful sunsets often presented, stopping many in their tracks in admiration. After our evening meal we sat in the light of kerosene lamps, sipping our beer or whisky, and generally unwinding.

Supplies were now generous, the source close at hand at Dimapur, and the metalled road fairly stable in the dry season. That is, not being washed down the steep hill side, following a heavy tropical rain downpour of some 5-6 inches.

For recreation some read or wrote letters home, others played cards, or a game devised by our group called Lie-Dice. This used dice, together with covering leather cups, and heaps of bluff, encouraged by minor small bets! We soon became expert at the game.

Then to bed, a camp bed in tent with blanket to ward off the chilly night air at 4000 feet. Altogether, quite a pleasant interlude between two very strenuous and bitter campaigns, with heavy cost to life and limb.

The Three Musketeers. Three officers and Naga hills clearly in the background.

Our Commanding Officer was Lt. Col. John Brierley and our Padre, Capt. Fr. Fitzgibbon, both having survived the Kohima campaign. Father Fitz, as he was known in the Mess, was in his forties, and was now recalled to base duties on account of age.

He was devastated, having developed a close relationship with the Worcesters, but orders are orders and we lost him.

Captain Pulido (FR Pulido) was his younger replacement, and looked after us throughout the coming campaign. Shortly before this, Lt. Col. Brierley was promoted to another area of the Division. We felt this was a loss to the Battalion, the timing could have been better. His replacement was Lt. Col. Charles Street.

CHAPTER FOURTEEN

Action – Burma Campaign

Maram–Tamu–Kelewa–Ye-u–Shwebo–Ava–Mandelay–
Legyi, Mt. Popa

November 29th 1944

O ur rest, rehabilitation, reinforcement, and training interlude
was now over.

Our reinforcements had been drawn from within the division,
from disbanded anti-aircraft units, transport, and other units, not
now required at full strength. For some of these men, training as
infantrymen came hard, but by dispersing them amongst our
sections they had the support and guidance of experienced Worcester veterans close around them.

They did well in the coming campaign.

As Regimental Medical Officer, (R.M.O.) I had total use of a
jeep fitted to carry two loaded stretchers. It had a towing bar for
a trailer loaded with essential medication, splints, bandages, etc.,
required for the coming action.

My team consisted of:

Sgt. Middleton.
Cpl. Greenow.
Pte. Gore.
Pte. Yeomans and many others.

Sadly after 50 years, I cannot recall their names, although I remember them well. All of them fulfilled multiple roles, medical
orderlies, stretcher bearers and at times infantry riflemen, guarding

our wounded and ourselves. Throughout the campaign, my team proved to be efficient, loyal, and sterling indeed.

29th November

Our battalion was transported by divisional vehicles to Imphal, then on to Palel, through the Kabaw Valley, past Tamu to Kalewa.

During this journey, following the cessation of monsoonal rains, and high temperatures prevailing, the thick clinging mud of the Kabaw Valley road-track had turned to a fine powdery dust. This dust, churned up by the wheels of our vehicles, penetrated everywhere, choking all personnel.

At Kalewa our 2nd division was to take over the lead from the 11th East African division which had relieved us at Tamu, some weeks ago in time and some 150 miles in distance.

The 11th had driven the Jap forces past Kalewa, and had established a firm bridgehead over the Chindwin River.

Kalewa 19th December 1944

Our 5th Brigade, including the Worcesters, crossed the Chindwin at this point, via a 1200 foot long Bailey Bridge. This bridge had been constructed and set on floating pontoon by our engineers the R.E.s and the R.I.E.s, a brilliant feat.

Our line of supply was now extended, to conserve petrol we had to substitute all but a few essential vehicles for mule transport. We also had to emulate the mules in carrying our heavy packs on the march. Each battalion was allocated some 50 mules, with an additional attached R.I.A.S.C. company of 60 mules, with their Indian handlers to ferry our supplies, mainly food and ammunition.

The mules attached to each battalion were looked after and guided by Battalion personnel. These consisted of drivers of trucks and carriers dispossessed of their vehicles by the exigencies of the coming campaign. Known familiarly as Muleteers, they became very attached to their four legged, sometimes capricious charges.

When the tactical situation demanded, further supplies were dropped to us from the air. These drops were made from Dakotas D.C.3s, and commandos piloted by R.A.F. and U.S.A.F. Officers and men.

We owe them a great deal.

The Jap forces were now falling back, it was essential to keep them on the move to prevent their tactical regrouping. Speed was essential. We marched during the night to avoid the heat of the day, and the uncomfortable fall in night temperature, with dew dripping from the jungle canopy overhead.

Kaduma. We broke out of the jungle here, on to the plains of Northern upper Burma. Scorched by the summer sun the plains were hot and arid, with blinding sunshine after the jungle gloom.

Our objectives were the Kabo Weir, the town of Ye-U and its airfield, and to cross the M.U. river.

This was where the Japs were expected to make their next stand. Our sister battalion, the Dorsets were given the task of capturing Ye-U, with flanking help from the Worcesters and the Camerons. Artillery and air support, bombing and strafing were laid on, together with help from our tanks.

January 2nd 1945

Ye-U was captured, a bridgehead was established over the River M.U., the Kabo Weir captured intact and the enemy forces in retreat.

January 5th

In one of their rare appearances on this front, the R.A.F. and U.S.A.F. squadrons having swept the sky of their planes, a squadron of Jap Oscars appeared and bombed the Ye-U bridgehead.

They failed to destroy the one remaining bridge over the M.U. River.

Bailey Bridge over the Chindwin at Kalewa. The longest bridge in the world under construction

The Ava Bridge over the Irrawaddy. Blown by 17th Indian Division on the with-drawal from Burma, April, 1942

The Chindwin and The Irrawaddy Rivers. Reproduced by permission of the Imperial War Museum, London.

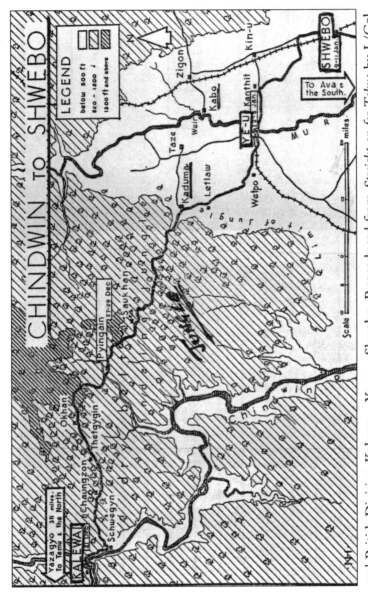

2nd British Division Kelewa – Ye-u – Shwebo. Reproduced from *Straight on for Tokyo* by L/Col. O.W.G. White, D.S.O. drawn by Captain Norman Havers, M.B.E.

January 6th.

As leading battalion at this time we Worcesters were crossing open paddy fields when the Oscars returned, a dozen in all. There were no anti-aircraft guns and no cover, we fell flat and buried our faces in the earth, praying hard.

The Oscars dropped antipersonnel bombs at will, then strafed us with cannon and machine gun fire, making several such passes. I kept, as souvenirs of the occasion, a spent cannon shell case and a machine gun bullet extracted from the soil beside me.

By some miracle, perhaps as a response to the fervent prayers of several hundred Worcesters, casualties were very light. Several ongoing skirmishes with the retreating Jap forces followed, culminating in an attack, spearheaded by the Worcesters, on a brigade scale, against the city of Shwebo.

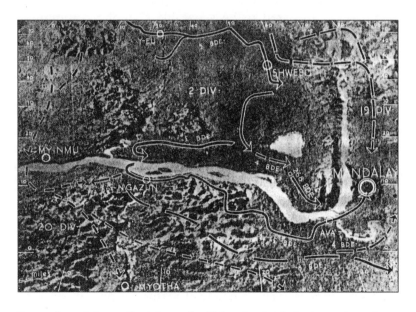

Reproduced from *Straight on for Tokyo* by L/Col. O.W.G. White, D.S.O. Drawn by Captain Norman Havers, M.B.E.

Shwebo was captured on 9th January, the largest city north of the Irrawaddy, with vital road and rail connections, together with its airfields.

A major prize, following advance of 130 miles in 19 days from Kalewa. Apart from battle casualties, this campaign was taking its toll. A steady stream of 4–5 men a day were falling sick, a severe drain on our already diminished manpower.

With 5th Brigade firmly established in Shwebo, a brigade of 19 Indian Division was busy disrupting the Jap withdrawal to the south, towards the Irrawaddy.

We were surprised to receive a deputation from the nearby village of Kandaw, a clean village and one of the few untouched by the war. Their leader enquired whether we had a Catholic priest available to celebrate Mass. They had not had the services of a priest for some years. Although most Burmese are Buddhist by religion, there appeared to be a sizeable Catholic community in and around the village. It was a solemn emotional occasion as our priest, Father Pulido, celebrated Mass in their simple church. Following the Mass we were offered tea and cakes and tried to answer their many questions, put so politely, about current world affairs.

In our role as infantry, at the cutting edge of the chisel, this was a rare social contact with the Burmese people. It was a pleasant feeling to be welcomed and to be able to converse with them, they were educated and spoke good English. Onward again, harassing the Jap forces towards the Irrawaddy, some 14 miles to the south.

Maundaung February 8th 1945

Here our three battalions came together some 5000 yards due north of the Irrawaddy.

Our 5th Brigade was now spread across a front of some 7500 yards, close to but out of sight of the Irrawaddy, in preparation for its crossing.

A deception plan had been prepared to draw the Japs away from our crossing points.

2 Div was to lie low around the Maundaung area, while Units some miles to the east, were to make themselves seen and to create activities suggestive of a build up of forces in preparation for an attack on Saigaing, a city north of the bend in the Irrawaddy. (Please consult the map).

Our real objective was to effect a crossing of the Irrawaddy some miles to the West, then to swerve East and attack from the south-west. This would have the main Jap forces on the wrong side of the river, some 1800 yards wide at this time of the year.

Dawete, Tadaing, and Myitha were the jumping off points for the crossing by the Worcesters and the Camerons, where their forward companies were already deployed. The Dorsets were in reserve at Maundaung.

Our 2 Div. crossing was planned in conjunction with other units' crossings of the Irrawaddy, as follows:

Irrawaddy Crossing – (1945)

(1)   2 British Div.: (Cross Keys Insignia)

Crossing on 24–25th February, at Dawete, Tadaing and Myitcha, west of Sagaing, attacked and captured Ngazun and onwards.

(2)   20 Indian Div.: (Scimitar)

After capturing Monya on 22 January pushed south on our right flank to capture Myinmu and to establish a firm bridgehead fierce fighting resulted, with final break through to Kyaukse, and onward.

(3)   7th Indian Div.: (Arrow)

Captured Pakokku below the junction of the Chinwin and the Irrawaddy, and established a firm bridgehead on the 14th February. It was through this bridgehead, on 18th

February that 17th Indian Div., black cat insignia, passed in its charge to capture Meiktila, using motorised transport and tanks.

(4)   19th Indian Div.: (Dagger)

Crossed the Irrawaddy east of Swebo on the 14th January, established a bridgehead, strongly opposed by the Japs. Broke through and fought its way south to capture Mandalay (20 March).

'The best laid plans o' mice and men gang oft a'gley'. So it was in our particular sector on the night of 7/8th February 1945.

A strong force of Japanese soldiers silently crossed the Irrawaddy in partial moonlight, and bumped into a platoon of B company, the Worcesters, guarding Tadaing village. The Jap force surged forwards first cutting, then following the field service telephone wire to Dawete village. There, they attacked the other 2 platoons, under command of Major Tooby, putting in several fierce attacks, between darkness and dawn. These attacks were repulsed by the Worcester garrison, which was still holding firm by dawn's light.

At daybreak, our commanding officer, Lt. Col. Charles Street realised that his forward platoons were pinned down by enemy machine gun fire. He ordered an immediate counter-attack with his A and C rifle companies. Personally leading the attack, he was killed, together with several Officers and Men in driving the Japs out of their forward positions. Amongst those severeley wounded were one Officer, one N.C.O., and one soldier, each sustained bullet wounds of the thigh, resulting in a compound fracture of the femur. Three such wounds, sustained at the same time, would strongly suggest they were caused by machine guns firing on fixed lines. In World War I, this type of injury carried a mortality of up to 70 per cent in the Flanders mud, because of difficulty of evacuation of casualties. Here, the wounded were rapidly carried to our near-by R.A.P.. We gave them transfusions of plasma and intravenous anaesthetic, to sedate, relieve their pain and spasm,

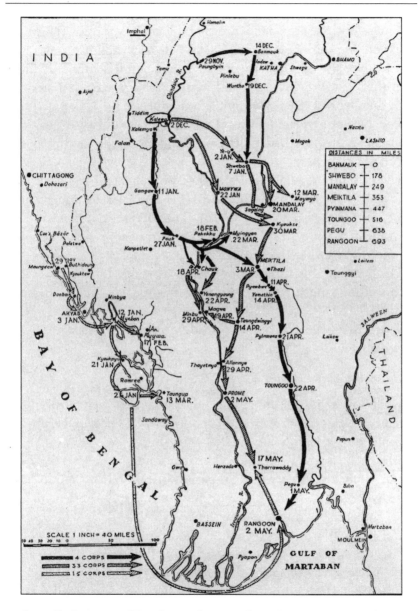

Overall Strategy. "Breakout from Kelewa." Reproduced from
S.E.A.C. Souvenir published by Frank Owen (1945).

and to allow cleaning and dressing of their wounds. This was followed by splints and traction in Thomas Splints, and rapid transfer, via the M.D.S., to the advanced surgical unit. All three men survived. For my team and myself, a harrowing and anxious time, but with a deeply satisfying outcome.

The Dorsets, ordered forward to relieve our forward positions found that the Japs had pulled out, and promptly occupied the vacant slit trenches.

The two forward companies of the Worcesters moved back into reserve to lick their wounds and to get reorganised, under command of our new C.O., Lieut Col. Tom Irvine, transferred to us from the Camerons. The crossing of the Irrawaddy was scheduled for the night of 24th February.

The river at this time of the year was some 1800 yards wide, with shifting sandbanks and a current of some 4-5 knots, no mean obstacle.

Worcester were to be the leading battalion, starting point Dawete, time 23.00 hours.

Night of the 24th February

Alas, almost a full moon! Using infantry assault craft of doubtful vintage (collapsible canvas and wood), the Worcesters began the crossing of the Irrawaddy.

Surprise was lost when the outboard motors were started, some of the old boats, heavily loaded, began to leak, fill and sink. Other boats were holed by machine gun fire from the opposite bank and sank with their wounded. Our newly arrived C.O. Col. Irvine, found himself swimming, sustained an accidental kick to his head from a heavy boot of one of the struggling swimmers, but managed with many others to reach the north bank safely.

Our sister Battalion, the Camerons, starting from Myitha fared better, getting over a Company, which included their C.O. (Lt. Col. McAlester).

By noon on the 25th they had the remainder of the Battalion across, but not without casualties and the sad loss of their R.M.O., Captain Peter Barkey.

The Dorsets had now achieved a crossing, followed by the Worcesters, and a battle regrouping began, prior to an attack on the Japanese positions at Ngazun. This was to be a two battalion frontal attack, parallel with the Irrawaddy on the left, and an open flank on the right.

March 7th 1945

The attack on Ngazun was preceded by an air strike by Hurricanes and Lightnings followed by heavy artillery barrage. Bayonets fixed, Worcesters and Dorsets advanced at increasing pace, a fearsome sight for the enemy. Twenty-five pounder shells were landing on Ngazun positions, 3.7 anti-aircraft shells, from distant guns, bursting in the air to our front sounding like giant whips wielded by Brobdingnags.

There was no going back, onward one and all, our few casualties we carried, or they walked forward intermingled with the tail of the battalion. One's adrenalin flowed freely, a high resulted, excitement, not fear, shouting from sheer exhilaration as we participated in the advance on Ngazun.

Ngazun taken with few casualties, mopping up began of enemy forces in the area.

One of the better things of war in Assam and Burma was that the local inhabitants seemed to have an instinctive appreciation of where the action would be, they faded away in good time to safer areas. Our 5th Brig. now in reserve for a few days, with the Irrawaddy close at hand, bathing and washing of clothes was organised, and letters home, long overdue, were written. Meanwhile our 4th and 6th Brigade continued the chase. On the move again, Worcesters and Camerons in the lead.

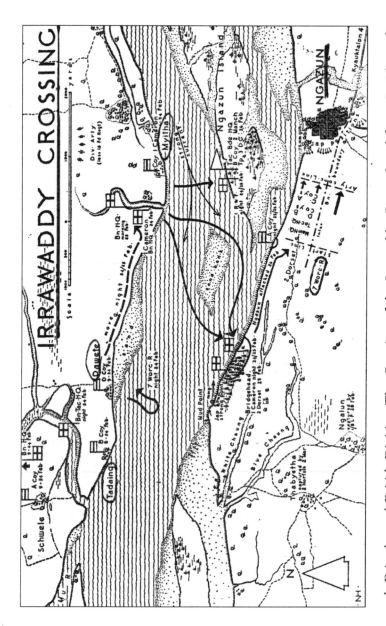

5th Brigade, 2nd British Division The Crossing of the Irrawaddy. Reproduced from *Straight on for Tokyo* by Lt/Col. O.G.W. White, D.S.O. drawn by Captain Norman Havers, M.B.E.

<u>Kyauktalon</u>: Worcesters were halted by enemy fire, from strongly held positions.

March 9th

Worcesters attacked the position at dawn coming under heavy enemy fire. Terrain difficult for infantry movement and impossible for tanks. Camerons on our left fared no better.

Night attack March 10th. Dorsets chosen, given difficult task, to hook through and get behind the Jap positions. With artillery support and great determination they captured the vital area at and around Dirty Pagoda, thus opening the road to the South.

The Dorsets suffered heavy casualties, their wounded being treated by their R.M.O Captain Joe Chamberlain, later awarded the M.C. Evacuation of the wounded was greatly assisted by the use of armoured ambulances and Bren carriers, in their transport to the M.D.S., and then flown out by L.5s., light planes modified to carry wounded.

Whilst the Dorsets were carrying out this attack, the Worcesters had captured Letpanzin, and made for U-Yin, the Camerons making for the defences of Ava.

The summer sun beat down, fierce and unrelenting, with little shade available. The ground dry and scorched, the many large rocks too hot to touch. (Burma's Dry Zone) Marching with heavy packs, weapons and ammunition then fighting, was exhausting to all ranks. Dehydration, heat exhaustion and fatigue had to be combated, scratches from thorn bushes turned septic and were slow in healing.

Fever from malaria, picked up in the Kabaw Valley, breaking through the Mepacrine barrier, had to be differentiated from heat exhaustion, and promptly treated. Also present was persistent diarrhoea, troublesome to many.

The battalion having covered some 250 miles from Kelewa on the Chindwin, most of it on foot, was near exhaustion.

I felt it right to report this to our Commanding Officer Lt. Col. Tom Irvine who discussed this matter with our Brigadier Michael West.

A short respite was given us, to rest, rehydrate, and ready ourselves for the next action.

March 17th 1945

Action again, the Camerons captured the moated defences of Ava, the Worcesters advancing through them towards the Myitnge River, crossing with little opposition to reach the east end of the Ava bridge, then deploying south of Hmandan Fort. Dorsets then passed through the Worcesters to set up a road block across the Kyaukse road, and to shoot up retreating enemy vehicles.

Meanwhile, far to our right General Messervy and his 4th Corps, spearheaded by the 17th Indian Div., passed through the bridgehead gained by 7 Indian Div. They went hell for leather, with their motorised troops and tanks, a blitzkrieg ignoring Jap forces on their flanks to reach Meiktila.

This bold move effectively cut the Japanese forces in two leaving their northern portion isolated.

Fierce fighting followed in the Meiktila area, especially for the control of its airfield.

March 27th 1945

Short period in reserve ended for the 5th Brigade. We were bussed some 80 miles to Myingyan at the junction of the Chindwin and Irrawaddy rivers.

Journey hot and dusty, with halts to deal with roving small Jap parties, but how nice to get a lift at last!

Logistics – The Art, Science, and Methods of Supply.

Napoleon's dictum: 'An army marches on its stomach'

This was now evident, we were outstripping our supplies, despite extremely efficient land, rail, river, and air means of their delivery.

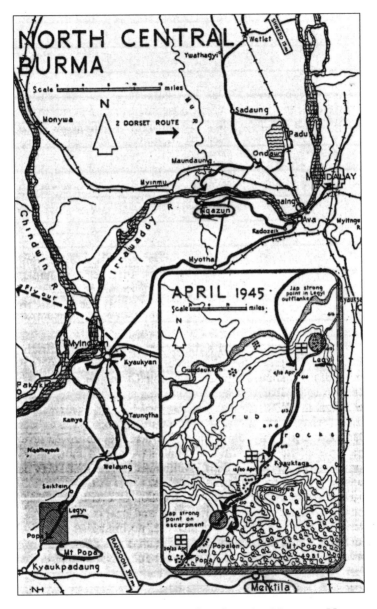

On to Mount Popa (drawn by Captain Norman Havers
M.B.E.)

It was decided at G.H.Q. that 2 Div. and 36 Div., containing the largest group of British troops, were the most demanding of supply, and were to be flown back to India.

A leaner group was to continue to pursue the Japs to Rangoon some 400 miles to the south and attempt to do so before onset of the monsoonal rains. First though, 2 Div. had to capture Legyi and the Mount Popa bastion dominating the road to the south, and so open up the road.

Worcesters advanced to M.S.417, (Miles from Rangoon now), the Camerons held up at Legyi, after repulse by determined resistance of Jap forces in strong position dominating the road.

April 4th 1945.

Worcesters moved around enemy's right flank, taking up positions behind him.

Dorsets passed through us to cut the road south of the Jap positions.

Heavy artillery fire from the Japs, 150 and 105 mms. shells falling close. This they kept up daily during our advance to Mt. Popa. Japanese resistance at Legyi was stubborn, but was taken by a determined early morning attack by the Camerons, on 9th April, with support from the Worcesters.

Onward to Mt. Popa, some 6000 ft. in height, arising from the immense Popa Massif, itself some 1000 feet above the surrounding plain. Two villages, Popa and Popalong lay on this plateau.

Worcesters moved forward under the Massif, our artillery together with the brigade mortars, under command of Captain Potter of the Worcesters, kept up a steady fire on the enemy's position. 'Jitter-parties' of Japs kept us alert at nights, and their shelling intensified, using up their ammunition in their determined rearguard resistance. Our R.A.P. seemed to get its full share of the heavy shelling, most intense on the night of 19th April. We were straddled by 150 and 105 mm shells landing close by our R.A.P.

with fragments of shells and pieces of the rocky ground whizzing unpleasantly close.

There was little we could do but to sweat it out and cope as best we could in treating our casualties. Our team did good work.

Air raids and heavy shelling combined with advances towards Popa finally resulted in the Jap abandoning their positions and retreating southwards.

Our Vanguard shortly after made contact with Units of 268 brigade advancing towards us from the south, the road was now open and our task completed.

April 23rd 1945

Following our divisional advance of some 800 miles from Dimapur, much of it on foot, our long journey back to India began.

From Myingyam we emplaned in Dakotas (D.C.3 aircraft), landing at Chittagong in Bengal, then by train to Bandel, hot, steamy, and mosquito ridden.

Rangoon had now fallen to our combined forces bringing the campaign in Burma to a successful conclusion – bar essential mopping up in the Pegu-Yomas area. The monsoonal rains now broke in real earnest.

June 1945

Our brigade, 5th, moved to an all-weather basha camp at Kamereddi some 60 miles north of Secondrabad. This was to be our camp for the next few months. Rest and recreation, refitting and further training to prepare us in readiness to join forces in the recapture of Malaya.

The Atom bomb, followed by the surrender of Japan, altered this situation.

This resulted in 2 Div. being separated into two groups:

(1)   Personnel – due for return to the U.K. and demobilisation. (Many had served 4 years overseas already).

(2)   Personnel – chosen to form the new BritJap Force 152, to
represent British and Commonwealth occupation forces in
Japan. In the process, 2nd. Div. was to lose nearly all its
remaining key personnel to form BritJap-Force, a full
strength revitalised 5th Brigade.

This Brigade consisted of the following Battalions: 2 Dorsets –
including reinforcements of 150 Worcesters and 400 Gloucesters.
1 Camerons. 2 Royal Welsh Fusiliers.

BritJap Force was officially formed on the 15th September 1945,
and was based at Nazik near Bombay, whilst awaiting its deploy-
ment to Japan. Personnel for repatriation to the U.K. were to
await their draft call at Kamereddi, and their service documents
brought up to date.

Daily groups of 5–10 men were paraded to the R.A.P. for full
medical examination, recording of sickness and wounds sustained
during the long campaign.

As their R.M.O., this task fell to me and sometimes took all
day to complete. I was happy to be of such service to them but
I became progressively saddened by the daily loss of familiar faces,
Officers, N.C.Os, and men of the Worcesters.

Companions with whom I had served, endured, and suffered
throughout the arduous campaign.

As their R.M.O. I had looked after their health, and tended
their wounds and now they were fast disappearing and leaving me
behind – sad, sad days!

I could see no future in my pending posting to base areas,
performing routine medical duties, surrounded by peacetime spit
and polish regulations.

Out of the blue came a letter from Joe, my friend and colleague,
Captain Joe Chamberlain, M.C.

Joe had been R.M.O. to the Dorsets in France (1939–40), in
India during training days, and throughout the Assam-Burma
Campaign.

Final objective of 5th Brigade. *Mount Popa*. Burma's Day Zone. 'Hot, arid, dusty.' (1945) Photograph by courtesy of the Imperial War Museum.

Commanding Officers 5th Infantry Brigade. 7th Worcesters: Lt.Col. T.A. Irvine. 2nd Dorsets: Lt.Col. O.W.G. White. 1st Camerons: Lt.Col. A.J.J. Somervile McAlester. Our commanding Officer Lt.Col. Tom Irvine, D.S.O. (on right of picture). Produced by permission of the Imperial War Museum.

As one of the longest serving Medical Officers in 2 Div. Joe was due for repatriation and demobilisation, and therefore not eligible to accompany his Dorsets to Japan. Instead he found himself posted as temporary R.M.O., to a Royal Marine Regiment based at Mahd Island, in the Bombay area, whilst awaiting his repatriation home.

Joe asked me whether I would exchange places with him, I agreed.

Joe must have pulled some powerful strings, for within a few days I found myself posted to the Royal Marine Regiment.

CHAPTER FIFTEEN

The Royal Marines

THE 34TH ROYAL MARINE AMPHIBIOUS REGIMENT was based at Mahd Island in the Bombay area.

I was posted to them, as their R.M.O., on September 5th 1945. At the request, nay order of their C.O., 'You're one of us now', I exchanged my khaki head gear for their blue beret and wore it with some pride. The Marines were also caught unawares by the sudden and unexpected Japanese surrender.

Here they were, recently out of England, young ready and able, bursting to take part in amphibious operations in the recapture of Malaya and suddenly the switch was turned off!

Their C.O. was naturally keen to achieve some action and very soon we embarked for Batavia (now Jakarta) to assist in control of civil unrest, rife since the Japanese surrender.

Our first port of call was Singapore where we replenished supplies, including anti-mosquito sprays and ointments and water sterilising tablets and powders. There was no shore leave.

Our ship was not built for the tropics, the hot steamy atmosphere aboard being most evident at night in the cabin. Most of us slept on deck where the air movement was a blessed relief.

On arrival at Batavia the situation was chaotic, with political flak flying, fortunately over our heads, between British, Dutch and Indonesian authorities, as to how and who should be governing locally.

Within a few weeks we received orders recalling the Regiment to Mahd Island. Evidently our Regiment was considered too highly specialised and too valuable to be used for this type of police ground operations. We were happy with this decision.

The next few months with the Marines on Mahd Island were happy ones, taking daily sick parades inspecting camp kitchens, and sanitation.

Commonly seen at each Sick Parade were those suffering from Tropical Ear and various skin conditions, notably Dhobi-Itch, a form of fungus infection of the skin of the groin and axilla, first cousin as it were to the better known Athlete's foot.

Prickly Heat proved troublesome, often resistant in the hot moist atmosphere, and at times necessitating its victim a short spell at a nearby hill station where the cool dryer weather aided its cure.

My afternoons were largely free except for the occasional accident or sudden acute illness. The Marines had converted one of their many assault craft into a seagoing ambulance. It had stretchers as bunks, cupboards for medicines, dressings, etc., space and table for surgical operations. There was room for over 20 casualties at any time.

On several occasions, when things were quiet in camp, we (our team) took our ambulance to sea. It was driven by a powerful engine at a good 10 knots. We practised the usual manoeuvres and procedures of the handling and treatment of potential casualties, although the need for this was fast receding. The assault craft had originally been armed with a flame thrower situated at its bow. This had not been dismantled and could still be energised. Just once we tried it out, – Wow! A stream of liquid flame soared in a high arc some 20 yards to our front, burning fiercely throughout its length and continuing to burn on the sea surface.

I shudder to visualise its effects on the human body and was very glad that there was now no need for its use. During most afternoons, for those members not on duty or on jankers, 'Charpuoy drill' was permitted from 13–15.00 hours, a siesta during the hot afternoon and a popular one. Now well established with the

C.O. and Adjutant, I was granted weekend leave to visit my
Worcester friends who now formed part of BritJap Force stationed
at Nasik only a two hour drive from Bombay.

I took my driver and batman, we covered the miles easily on
a good road, and arrived at Marabout Lines, the tented camp of
the Dorsets. The Dorsets, you might remember, now had some
150 Worcesters absorbed into their battalion.

I was happy to meet them again, my former comrades in arms,
and to talk over old times and present times. Amongst their Officers
was Captain Harry Parton, M.C., one of my friends from the
Worcesters, who unknowingly some time in the future was to be
best man at my wedding. We spent a pleasant 24 hours as their
guests, before returning to Mahd Island, and back to work.

Some weeks later, the Officer Commanding a nearby Unit
whose medical side I was looking after, sent for me. He requested
that I accompany his Adjutant and himself to inspect a bordello
popular with some of his officers, and those of surrounding units.
It was locally known as the 'Officers' Club'!! The CO. wished to
ascertain whether the establishment was clean and properly managed. With safety in numbers as it were, we sallied forth, but not
regardless.

Madame greeted us on arrival and seemed confident that her
establishment would pass muster – 'I keep a clean house'. The
foyer led into a very large room, carpeted and quietly decorated,
with some half dozen rooms, with closed doors, leading from it.

The lighting was soft, the atmosphere relaxed, turbanned waiters
were serving drinks, especially Scotch Whisky, at exorbitant prices.
Anyone walking in, after passing the close scrutiny of the Sikh
doorman, would imagine he was entering the foyer of a respectable
hotel.

Led by Madame, a well dressed and well preserved Anglo-Indian
lady, we inspected some of the side rooms leading off the main
room, 'The others are in use you understand.' The side rooms

were small and clean with bed made up, cupboard, dressing table and an ensuite for use 'before and after'. Sheets and pillow cases were changed after each client, Madame insisted, each girl had her own room. Madame also assured us that each of her girls has a regular medical examination, 'I run a clean house.' The girls were young, attractive and well dressed, attentive yet allowing their future clients to look around and in their own time make their choice of partner. They meanwhile encouraged them to buy the house drinks, again at exorbitant prices. Madame had trained them well. A Conference with the C.O. and Adjutant produced a unanimous verdict – 'A clean well-run house.'

We sat down in comfortable armchairs and ordered Scotch whisky, Scotch being almost unobtainable elsewhere. It proved to be the genuine article. The reader by now will almost certainly be asking this question, 'Did they, or did they not?' To any warm blooded man, it can be said that the temptation was there.

Apart from the moral issues involved, my medical training gave me fair warning of the possible consequences of the social diseases.

This was summed up by one of our teachers, at the Royal Infirmary – 'An hour with Venus, then a lifetime with Mercury.' So I enjoyed the Scotch!

The Marine Regiment was by now being affected by events occurring in south-east Asia. No real task for its special skills, no seaborne operations, it was now in limbo. Its recall to Britain appeared imminent.

In view of this coming event and the strong possibility of my being returned to routine base duties, I volunteered for posting to Civil Affairs Services S.E. Asia, with a preference for Burma, or Malaya.

The massive disruption of civil services and administration during the Japanese occupation of S.E. Asia required urgent attention. To fill this gap, the loss of so many civil servants, doctors, engineers, etc., a call for Volunteers from the Armed Services was made.

This was intended as an urgent measure, using qualified personnel already in the area to get things moving. Meanwhile I applied for leave, three weeks, to see my parents who had retired to a hill station, called Kotagiri situated in the Nilgiri Hills.

By train and bus journey I arrived at Kotagiri, to find my parents in good health. My parents had decided, on retirement, to spend some time at Kotagiri, whilst the rush home was at its peak.

Shipping space was limited, and the numbers large, women 4 to a cabin, men 4 to 6, husbands and wives separated for the journey, crowded decks, and crowded meals, etc. My Father as an ex-ships' officer, would have none of this, and opted to wait until the 'rush' was over.

Dad, Mum and I had a pleasant time together at Kotagiri. It would be nearly three years before we met again. Back with Marines at Mahd Island, my posting to 'Civil Affairs' arrived, I was to report to their Head Quarters at Pallavaram.

Pallavaram was virtually a large staging camp, holding the many various groups pending their onward movement to their selected destination. After the discipline of Army life the local situation appeared chaotic, but things were soon sorted out.

I found myself in charge of a group of a dozen men and women, civilians bound for Malaya. After a long train trip, then a longer sea journey, we found ourselves at Singapore. Having assisted in sending off my charges to their various destinations, I entrained for Kuala Lumpur to report for further orders and posting.

CHAPTER SIXTEEN

Civil Affairs – Malaya

H.Q. Kuala Lumpur
March 1946

A SCOTTISH COLONEL WAS IN CHARGE of Medical Admini-stration, himself a civilian doctor in uniform.

He examined my dossier carefully, raised an eyebrow or two and then said, 'What is it you want to do, laddie?'

'Sir,' I replied, 'I would like to be posted up country to a civilian hospital where I can practise real medicine.'

'Is that so, laddie?' he replied walking over to a large wall map, pointed to Kuala Lipis, and said, 'Is that far enough for you?'

And so I joined a military convoy; after some hours over twisting roads, through jungle country, we arrived at Kuala Lipis. I found myself sharing a government house with a forestry officer.

Next day I reported to the hospital, which consisted of a two storey stone block and multiple pavilion style wards around it with pleasant green surrounds. A hospital of some 150 beds, including a children' ward and a maternity ward, operating theatre male and female wards, and a T.B. isolated section. There was also a small laboratory where blood was daily examined for malarial parasites, stools for Helminths, etc.

Dr Menon was in charge, he had run the hospital single handed throughout the Japanese occupation, after his European colleague was abruptly removed by the Japanese and placed in a P.O.W. camp.

Dr Menon and I hit it off right away, as also did Helen the

Matron, an Australian Nursing Sister. We made a good team, worked well together, and became firm friends. The staff, male and female, were recruited from the three main races in Malaya, namely Malay, Chinese and Indian. As I got to know them I found them friendly, courteous, and efficient.

The clinical work was intensely interesting and a contrast from the necessarily restricted scope of wartime Army medicine. The Japanese by their neglect had brought a trail of disorders to the people, malnutrition, avitaminosis, malaria, anaemia, beri-beri, and a host of secondary conditions from the above causes. Ulcers of the lower limbs were slow in healing, pulmonary tuberculosis increased, scabies rife, especially amongst the children.

Verily a Pandora's Box of troubles. Sometimes it was hard to know where to begin, to assess the priorities of treatment, where multiple disorders co-existed in the one patient. It soon became clear to me that irrespective of the conditions prevailing, the correction of malnutrition and avitaminosis was paramount. This was easier said than done, the hospital could feed its patients high protein diets, but not the town and the surrounding district. Vitamin pills could be given at our out-patient sessions, but no guarantee of their being taken.

Local folklore, I was told, tended to grade Western treatments in the following order:

Injections – Very good medicine

Mixture, especially nasty tasting ones – Fairly Good

Pills and Tablets – not so good.

For special conditions, such as acute beri beri, injections of Vitamin B.1 were freely given, but for the rest?

Many of the present medicines, wonder drugs, now taken for granted, were not then discovered.

We had the Sulpha drugs and basic penicillin (1946), which needed to be given by injection, since it was destroyed by the stomach juices.

Its short duration of action led to the need for injections to be given every three hours – Ouch!!

Another important fact I soon learned, and one also learned by those practising overseas:

'Work with Mother Nature, not against her, and she will work with you.'

Good asepsis, clean hands, sterile dressing and minimal interference, coupled with good diet and vitamins worked wonders.

Today's major hospitals with their plethora of drugs and too frequent interference with nature, might perhaps learn something here.

Another point of interest, in the Children's Ward no child was ever left alone. A relative, Mother, Aunt or elder sister, taking shifts, was always at the child's cot. The child was patted gently from time to time, talked to quietly, changed and fed.

Much later, in our Western world, the teachings of Dr John Bowlby emphasised this vital need of contact and companionship with the child, especially when in strange surroundings in hospital.

In order to communicate with my patients and with the general public, I began to learn Malay, the lingua franca of Malaya. Some 80% of the hospital staff spoke English, which made my first few months a lot easier. To ensure that I kept learning, I used to write out ten new words each night and paste the slip onto my shaving mirror. With the help of the Malay Guru (teacher) I found, after 3 months, that I was able to take a ward round and out-patient session in Malay.

To complicate things however, many of the Chinese and Indian labourers could only speak their respective dialects be it Cantonese, Hokkien, Tamil, etc. No real problem, most of my staff could speak more than one language, and several dialects. It was interesting to witness a common scene between interpreter and patient, both Chinese.

Nurse and patient would first look at each other, from facial characteristics trying assess their probable dialect. Nurse would begin with, say, Cantonese, patient reply in Hokkien, they would then agree on (say) Teocheo!!

Pahang is a large, virtually unspoiled state, with jungle and many rivers. The Pahang river, close to Kuala Lipis has many tributaries along which are numerous Malay Kampongs (Villages), many of which had had no contact with the Japanese. The Japs had no cause to venture far upstream, and the Malay villagers certainly avoided going down.

The villagers grew their own rice, fished the river, and remained in isolation during the occupation!

Unlike the town dwellers, malnutrition was not their major problem.

Now, some villagers were coming, sometimes long distances, to the hospital for treatment and also seeking medicines for their village. It became clear that considerable sickness was present in the kampongs.

Dr Manon, the Matron and I talked over this problem. We arranged to borrow a motorised perahu (canoe) from the local Public Works Department, together with a boatman. We equipped it for a long trip up and down the river loaded with medication and rations and of course enough spare petrol. I would be accompanied by a trained male Malay nursing assistant to help in the many areas, and situations to be encountered.

And so, off into the Ulu. We arrived at the first kampong after several hours chugging, to be greeted by the Pengulu, village headman, and his Elders. The villagers crowded the river bank, gazing with curiosity at the Tuan Doctor Puteh – white doctor, many of the children never having seen one before! Following the traditional greetings an open-air out-patient session was begun. Best to start with the children, who, following earlier distribution of glucose sweets, seemed to have lost their initial shyness. Flanked by a protective screen of parents and/or relatives, the children were brought forward for examination and treatment. With scarcely an exception, all were found to have scabies mites, the lesions most evident in the web of their fingers, where scratching had led to secondary infection. Most seemed also to have nematode infestation (round worms), and the enlarged spleen of chronic malaria.

New to me at this time was the disease known as Yaws, one which produced raised cauliflower-like lesions on the skin and when present on the soles of the feet made walking difficult and painful. A crab-like walk was the result, leading to the name Crab Yaws.

Fortunately these conditions mentioned, disorders and diseases, were treatable, medicines and ointments were given, with careful instructions and demonstrations in their use.

Time to move on to the next kampong, so with farewells of 'Salamat Jalan' from the villagers, and 'Salamat tinggal' from ourselves off we went. Following several such visits, darkness was approaching, and we were offered the use of a hut for the night. We unrolled our sleeping bags on to the floor, slung our mosquito nets, partook of our rations and slept well. Our river trip lasted over a fortnight, and was satisfying on several counts.

Firstly – We had made valuable contact with the villagers.

Secondly – We had treated their medical conditions.

Thirdly – The villagers would now feel encouraged to undertake the river trip to the hospital for treatment.

It was nice to learn at a later date that the villagers were both impressed by and appreciative of our efforts.

Kuantan, Pekan, and the Istana

One day at Kuala Lipis we received a phone call from Dr Gross, our S.M.O. stationed at Raub.

His Highness, the Sultan of Pahang, had telephoned Dr Gross to request a medical officer be sent urgently to Pekan to examine and treat one of the Sultan's grand children who had fallen ill.

Pekan is near Kuantan on the East Coast of Malaya, a day's drive from Kuala Lipis. I packed my medical bag and a few clothes and prepared the car for the journey.

Sandy, a young assistant Forestry Officer, with whom I shared a house, asked if he could accompany me, as he had not yet inspected this area of his Forestry responsibilities, and this would be a good opportunity to do so.

We set off at a modest pace and reached Kuantan safely. Having established a base at the Government bungalow at Kuantan, I drove on to Pekan where the Sultan's Istana (Palace) was situated.

There, following introductions, I was shown into the sick room containing the patient, a child of some 6 years of age. A short history of the illness, and a physical examination, led to a diagnosis of measles, a fairly severe attack, with hundreds of spots. Some bronchitis was present, as well as the usual conjunctivitis, but fortunately no severe complications. Reassurance was given, together with nursing instructions, cough syrup, and a little sedative for night time.

I visited daily for one week, to ensure all was going well. I was glad to find that my conversational Malay was fluent enough to make myself understood to mother, child and the many attentive relatives. Before leaving, the family graciously allowed me to take photographs of themselves as a memento. My daily visits to the Istana were made during the midmorning, a convenient time for the family. Prior to these visits I called daily at the Government hospital at Kuantan, which was being looked after by a Chinese Matron and nursing staff of Malay, Chinese and Indians. In the early post-war period, there was as yet no medical officer, hence my summons to Pekan.

I was made welcome, and examined some of their patients whom they felt needed a doctor's opinion and advice. Following these daily visits the remainder of the day was free. Sandy and I took long walks, and swims, wonderfully clear water and white beaches. The beach was lined by many rows of coconut palms, and at intervals there were small Kampongs. Here we stopped to chat with the Malay Villagers and their children, and bought coconuts and freshly caught fish.

During one of my morning visits to the hospital, a boy of some 10 years was brought in to the Out-patients department accompanied by his father. He had sustained a deep cut to the palm of his hand some days ago, it was now heavily infected. On examination, the palm was ballooned and the finger already starting to flex towards the palm of the hand. The father and son were fishermen from one of the adjacent Indonesion Islands, tribally Bugis, isolated and having little contact with the outside, and practically no understanding of modern medicine. With the aid of one of the male nurses, I attempted to explain to the Father that the boy's palm needed incision to let out the bad fluid (pus).

This I could do now under a short ether anaesthetic. We got as far as the operating theatre, placed the boy on the table explaining to the Father as we went along. The theatre nurse gently put the face mask on the patient to administer the anaesthetic, this immediately caused distress and agitation to both father and son. Mask removed, I put it on to my own face to show that it did no harm and we tried once again. So far so good, son breathing steadily and father breathing even faster.

I swabbed the hand and palm with antiseptic solution, and reached for the scalpel and probe. 'Jaga'!!* cried the nurse, Father, wild eyed, was about to attack me. Perhaps, despite careful instructions, he thought that I was about to amputate his son's hand. I put down the scalpel and showed the Father my empty hand. Father grabbed his son from the operating table and ran away, both never to be seen again.

---

* Jaga = 'Look out' in Malay

Question, why did we allow the father into the operating theatre in the first place?

Answer, known to all who have practised abroad, because there was no chance at all of getting the boy into the theatre *without* his Father.

Sadly, the end result of not incising and draining the pus from the palmer space would result in a useless hand, the fingers flexed permanently into the palm.

This saddened me, so near and yet so far.

Overall, the week spent visiting the Istana, the hospital, and the beach and adjoining kampongs was a pleasant one. The miles and miles of spotless white sandy beach, the sparsely populated kampongs, the rows of coconut trees the small fishing boats, a tranquil setting.

I understand that Kuantan now, some fifty years later, has become a major tourist centre with 5 star hotels. Progress, or loss of something natural and beautiful?

The clinical work at the hospital at Kuala Lipis continued to be interesting and medically rewarding. The weeks flew by, soon my demobilisation number would be coming up. Some action must be taken if I were not to be whisked away:

(1) Letter to Senior Medical Officer, Pahang, volunteering to postpone my demobilisation for three months. (Dr Gross)

(2) Copy of this letter to Adjutant of Central Army H.Q.

(3) Formal application to join the Colonial Medical Service (Malaya), on demobilisation.

Replies from 1 and 2 favourable, from 3 'We are considering the matter.'

Shortly afterwards I was contacted by representatives of the Colonial Service who were now in Malaya interviewing prospective candidates for the Service. An appointment, and I fronted a group of three officials for a lengthy interview. I was informed by official letter that I had been accepted.

I also received a letter from my former Surgical Chief at Stirling Royal Infirmary, offering his congratulations on my being awarded the Military Cross, relating to my active service as R.M.O. to the Worcester Regiment during the campaign in Burma. (This was the first I knew of this award, being now out of touch with matters military).

[It was months later that I received a letter from H.M. King George, with citation and the Cross itself.] I made haste to the nearest military unit, their Adjutant consulted their latest *Military Gazette* and confirmed the award. I was deeply honoured to have my service so recognised. If only the award could have come through whilst I was still with my Worcesters. Several months later, now a civilian and member of the Colonial Medical Service (Malaya), I drove to Kuala Lumpur to discuss my immediate future with the Director of Medical Services (Malaya), namely Dr McGregor. He proved very helpful and agreed that after some 4 years overseas, I was due for home leave. Also that I was expected to attend and pass a 6 months' course at the School of Tropical Medicine in Liverpool, prior to my return to Malaya. I was happy with these decisions, and awaited events, whilst continuing clinical work at K/Lipis.

Some weeks later I received full instructions regarding my passage to England, leave period granted and dates of enrolment at the Liverpool School.

My luck seemed to be keeping up, I was young, still alive, active and with a future.

What more could one want?

CHAPTER SEVENTEEN

Return to Britain 1947

THE SEA VOYAGE HOME BEGAN PLEASANTLY, only four passengers to a cabin, and a comfortable passage for the returning
servicemen, ex-servicemen, and ex-servicewomen on board. We
passed through the Red Sea, hot and humid, then through the
Suez Canal, landing at Port Said. There we wandered around,
gazing at the many people of different races and dress, buildings
and shops. We also made the acquaintance of Simon Artz, a
world-famous large shopping complex, selling many varieties of
goods. Our ship then steamed into the Mediterranean, on to the
Straits of Gibraltar and entered the North Atlantic, heading for
home.

About a week prior to our arrival at Southampton, I experienced
a relapse of malaise and lowgrade fever. This had occurred during
the Burma Campaign despite which I soldiered on, as did many
others of my battalion. The symptoms worsened during the next
few days, leading to my consulting the Ship's Doctor who prescribed the usual medication. Things became worse with increasing
fever and nausea. I was transferred to the ship's sick bay for
observation and isolation from my companions. Not a good start
for my arrival in England!

I was to be examined by the Port Medical Officer on arrival,
together with some dozen other passengers in quarantine. I prepared myself for the worst. Two Port Medical Officers came aboard
to perform these precautionary examinations. They were especially
on the look out for persons with modified smallpox in part-immune
individuals. These persons would be highly infectious, although

often showing surprisingly little signs of illness. The Medical Officer examined me, excluding such exotic diseases, but said I should be isolated and kept under observation for a while.

At this very moment the other Medical Officer, having completed her share of the medical examinations, entered the room.

Once again I gazed into a pair of big brown eyes, and my heart missed a beat! The Medical Officer was Marie! We gazed at each other in silence for what seemed the space of a year. 'What are you doing here?' we both exclaimed. In short, I was shipped off to the Infectious Diseases Hospital, and guess who was the Doctor in charge – Dr Marie! I could not believe my luck, but would have preferred my reunion with Marie under more favourable circumstances. The next few days were comfortable ones, rest in bed, many tests, and best of all, regular visits by Dr Marie. My condition rapidly cleared up, on good medication, nursing, and 't.l.c.' I was discharged with a clean bill of health.

I booked accommodation at the Polygon Hotel and telephoned my parents. They had now retired and were resident in Guernsey. I arranged ship's passage to join them.

In the interval I called on Marie and we spent as much time as she could spare together. Marie was kept busy with many polio patients to look after, in addition to her other patients.

The long hot summer of 1947, somewhat rare in Britain, had led to an epidemic of poliomyelitis through most of the country. I was worried for Marie, she was right in the middle of things, without the protection of the Salk Vaccine, not available for some years yet to come. My anxiety was reinforced by the monotonous menacing creaking sound of several iron-lungs (Artificial Respirators) heard on each of my visits to the hospital.

Marie seemed unaware of the risks she was taking in her daily rounds attending to her polio patients. I kept my fears to myself.

Marie's annual leave fell due, her passage to Dublin already arranged, to join her parents, brothers and sisters resident there.

My passage to Guernsey was also arranged, but owing to earlier bookings by hordes of tourists no cabin accommodation was to be had. A storm on the way led to a miserable passage, cooped up in the State Room, unable to walk the deck because of rain and wind. Mum and Dad were there to meet me, a reunion after three years. I spent a lovely fortnight with them, weather now fine and sunny. I could not help telling them about Marie and of my eagerness to meet her again. They understood.

Sark – Channel Islands

The weather in Guernsey continued fine and the seas calm. Mum and Dad suggested that this would be a good time to visit Sark, to meet some of Mother's distant relatives and to see our ancestral homes. The Vaudins had lived there for centuries.

Grandma was a Vaudin and the family connection with Sark was real, if somewhat distant. The trip by ferry was uneventful, and the landing without mishap. In heavy seas it would have been somewhat hazardous. Our first impression was of steep high cliffs, and clear blue-green water. From high up on the cliffs, one could gaze down some hundreds of feet, into water fathoms deep and clearly see the bottom.

The island has its own local government, dating from Norman days, headed by the Dame of Sark (1947). Overall, the island comes under the aegis of the British government. Mother soon made contact with the Vaudins, made easier by her fluency in French.

The people of Sark speak English generally, and French from Norman sources. In addition they speak a patois, only understood by themselves. My fluency in French was gently tested, but could not compare with Mother's! Cousin Vaudin, (cousin many times removed), smiled and said to Mother, 'Il a oublié, il faut plus parler,' or words to that effect.

We had only a few hours to spend on Sark as the ferry was

soon to depart to return us to Guernsey. A lovely island, Sark, but isolated and too quiet for most people's fancy in 1947. It would require a drastic changed of lifestyle to reside there permanently, even if permission could be obtained.

I have often felt that I would like to make a return trip to Sark, to look up old Church and family records, and walk around and view its many historical attractions. Alas, too far, and too late! The return sea trip to Southampton was comfortable with fine weather.

I sought out Marie and took her to one of the popular tea-dances then available. She danced well and it was so nice to hold her.

A renewed courtship began. My feelings for Marie grew stronger day by day, I found myself hopelessly in love. When and how and where best to propose? One evening whilst we were sitting together in Marie's lounge, I expressed my love for her and asked her to marry me.

She said 'Yes'.

The next afternoon we walked around Southampton looking into jewellers' shops for an engagement ring. We finally decided on a beautiful ring of three blue-white diamonds, with the diamonds offset. I telephoned my parents to give them the good news, and Marie spoke a few words to them.

My leave was now at an end, time to entrain for Liverpool to begin my studies at the School of Tropical Medicine. A wrench to leave Marie.

The Colonial Office had booked accommodation for me, for six months at a large private house owned and run by a Miss Meredith in Ullet Road – Gracie, to her boys, (paying guests), an all male group of ex-service men, from each of the Services, studying for their various diplomas and degrees.

The house was a comfortable rambling three storey one with a large garden. It was situated right on the bus route to the school and close to an adjacent bus stop. Amongst the guests were two

Australian ex-service Doctors studying Orthopaedics. They were later to become top specialists in their field in Brisbane and one a close friend.

On arrival at the Liverpool School of Tropical Medicine, I found my way to the office and encountered a group of a dozen postgraduates waiting there. They were of varying age and nationality, which included students from Malaya, Iraq, India, Denmark, as well as from the U.K. and Ireland.

'Are we all here for the same purpose?' I asked.

'Yes, we are waiting to register for the course.' We became acquainted very quickly, and got on well together. We had a daily series of lectures and much emphasis was placed on sound microscopic technique and recognition of specimens. These were daily produced and demonstrated, plasmodia of malaria, ova of all three major helminths, etc. At other times many prepared slides greeted us, labelled only by code numbers for us to identify. Our chief microscopic demonstrator, David Dugnell, was an acknowledged expert in the field.

After minutes of searching our microscopic field without success, David would be called to assist – he always found the required organism with baffling ease!

David advised me regarding the purchase of a good microscope which I used throughout the course and which proved useful in my future work overseas.

I found that I was missing Marie very much and must have become a little despondent. This was picked up by my Mother when I telephoned her. Mother arrived out of the blue to cheer me up.

She stayed a few days at Gracie's with much benefit to me. Aren't Mothers wonderful! About halfway through my course I took advantage of a long weekend holiday to fly to Dublin to meet Marie's parents and to ask for her hand in marriage. Marie met me at the airport, and drove me to their home, Brookfield, where I met her parents, brothers and sisters.

We had dinner in an elegant dining room, the whole family was present. I tried to answer their questions as best I could and to give some assurance of my ability to look after their daughter. I was given a fair deal and later heard that Marie's Father was reported as saying, 'Maybe he'll do, I hope they will be lucky.' I hoped so too.

Back to studies, the weeks rolled by, frequent telephone calls to and from Marie. Obtaining a few days' leave from the hospital, Marie joined me in Liverpool, and we entrained for Edinburgh to stay with and meet Auntie Aggie and Cousin May. We dined at the Royal British Hotel, and caught up with news of the family abroad. Everything went well. Two days later, following a hearty Scottish breakfast, we caught the Flying Scotsman back to Liverpool, and Marie onward to Southampton.

The end of the course was nigh, and the exams too. Written and oral exams and very strict microscopic testing. The teaching had been of high standard and I had worked very hard.

Consequently I passed and obtained the Liverpool D.T.M. & H (Diploma of Tropical Medicine and Hygiene).

Arrangements for our coming wedding needed to be made, a quiet post-war one, with family and close friends. Marie took care of all the arrangements, including the most important, the church and the priest.

We received great help form her parish priest, Revd. Fr. O'Sullivan, and we were married at St Boniface Church Southampton. Bernard, Marie's elder brother, gave the bride away, Kay, her sister was bridesmaid, and Captain Harry Parton, M.C. was best man. Harry and I were both in uniform having obtained permission for the occasion from the War Office. It was a lovely wedding in sunny weather on 10 January 1948. The reception followed, then Marie and I, now husband and wife, took train to London for our honeymoon, staying at the Dorchester Hotel. Amongst other

Our Wedding Photograph

things, we saw *Annie get you Gun* and enjoyed the show, especially the lovely melodies heard for the first time. After only a week of our planned two weeks honeymoon, we were informed by the Colonial Office that two seats were available to Singapore on a Super Constellation Aircraft. Such seats being at the time as precious as gold we grabbed them!

January at London airport, it was snowing with a biting wind, Marie and Mother in fur coats, Dad and I muffled up with heavy woollen scarves and overcoats.

My parents had come all the way from Guernsey in such appalling weather to farewell us. In these days, passengers and their farewelling relatives could stay together almost to the steps of the plane. We bade my parents goodbye and entered the plane, a lovely four engined Super Constellation, with three distinctive tail rudders, the most modern passenger aircraft at this time. We were happy at the thought of warm weather and sunshine.

CHAPTER EIGHTEEN

Return to Malaya

COMFORTABLE SEATS AND A LONG FLIGHT TO CAIRO, staying overnight at the Heliopolis Hotel. We had dinner and dancing in a cosmopolitan atmosphere. It was interesting and enjoyable. We were awakened at 5 a.m. to prepare for our onward flight to Singapore, via Bombay. We slept well and awoke to bright sunshine, landing shortly after at Singapore Airport. We disembarked into tropical heat and humidity, Marie still wearing her fur coat to the amusement of all around.

We were met by Dr Lowson, the Principal Medical Officer, and his doctor wife. It appeared that they hoped that Marie would take charge of the Womens' and Children's Clinic at the General Hospital, Johore Bahru, as Dr (Mrs) Lowson was going on long service leave overseas. Marie was delighted as it was her particular interest. I was to take up duties as Medical Officer in charge of several wards, in addition to after-hours rostered duties for the whole hospital of 500 beds.

Whilst waiting for a Government House to become available we were housed in a comfortable apartment right at the top of the hospital, with views over the Straits of Johore and of Singapore Island. Our meals were served by an old Chinese retainer, who spoke little or no Malay, and little English.

He was friendly and helpful, we managed to communicate!

Marie and I rapidly entered into the local medical scene, enjoying our work and our relationship with the hospital staff and patients. Marie began lessons in Malay and I continued mine, she proved a good student.

Six months after our arrival in Johore sad news reached us by letter that Marie's Father had died suddenly, a great blow to her. There was nothing to be done, it was all over. Marie braved it out and put her energies into her work. A few weeks later a Government furnished house became available, one of the many fine houses owned by the Sultan, leased to the Government and sublet to us.

It was an imposing two storey stone building, with verandah, large rooms, car port and quarters for the servants. It had a beautiful garden. We moved in, heavy furniture was provided, we bought mattresses, sheets, crockery and cutlery, readily available at the many shops in Singapore. We engaged a Goanese cook-boy from the departing family, and settled in comfortably.

Dr Marjorie Lyon, was obstetrician in charge of the hospital's maternity wing. After 6 months in general medicine, I requested a transfer to Dr Lyon's wards and became her assistant. Dr Lyon was a highly qualified lady doctor, who had survived P.O.W. camp life. She was tough but fair and expected a high standard from all members of her staff. She was a very good teacher, with over 100 deliveries a month there was plenty of experience to be gained. Most of these deliveries were normal, carried out by the Sisters or Midwives, but there were many abnormal ones as well. These Dr Lyon handled herself until she was satisfied that I had developed the skill and judgement to cope with them. After 6 months with her tuition, I learned more in practical obstetrics than most registrars would have in 1–2 years elsewhere.

Our first daughter Joan-Marie was born in Johore, we nick-named her 'little blokkie'. In Malaya, the Government had an enlightened policy, as long as pregnant staff were fit and well, they were allowed to continue working. Marie worked until near term then went on maternity leave for 2 months. From an early age our little 'blokkie' was quite a Madam, active, curious, with a mind of her own! We obtained on excellent references, the services of a Chinese Amah (baby carer) to help to look after her. These Amahs form a traditional group, not nurses in the ordinary sense, but often widows with long experience of looking after children, starting with their own. Impeccably dressed, in white starched collared jacket, covering long black cotton trousers, hair neatly combed back in a bun, this was their uniform. We were fortunate in obtaining such efficient help.

The Drs Lowson had now returned from their long service leave, following which we were posted to Batu Pahat, a town some 80 miles up country. Myself in charge of the 150 bed hospital, Marie in charge of the Women and Children's Clinic in the town. Batu Pahat, like many of the towns in Malaya, was predominantly Chinese, with a minority of Indians and Malays. The major Malay population lived in the rural kampongs, many skirting the numerous tributaries of the many rivers. They used perahu (canoes) for transport, in the absence of proper roads, in many more remote areas.

Our catchment area of medical responsibility extended widely from the town and included an estimated population of some 150,000 people. Practising in the town itself were about half dozen Chinese, Malay and Indian general practitioners, as well as many traditional, non-medical ones. Our house was a pleasant stone bungalow, with verandahs, large rooms and servants' quarters at the rear. Our garden was surrounded by shoulder high grass which extended for some hundreds of yards. There was a long tarmac drive from the front door to the main road, leading to the hospital about a mile away.

From the departing family we inherited their cook-boy and their red setter bitch. This was the custom in those days, a responsibility was felt to ensure the ongoing employment of good servants, similarly with their domestic animals. The red setter's name was Trouble, but she gave us none, only her affection. Our Amah came with us from Johore to Batu Pahat, she was called Ah Quah, she was very loyal and we were very fond of her, she stayed with us during our two and a half years in Batu Pahat.

Apart from her Clinic in the town, Marie paid regular visits to the Government schools scattered around the rural areas to conduct medical examinations of the children, also to advise the teachers regarding general and specific public health measures, as found necessary. These rural excursions were to prove a source of worry to me.

100 cases of smallpox in village

Marriages are important events for families everywhere, none more so than in Malaya. Many of the families from a kampong not far from Batu Pahat, attended such a wedding held at one of the many adjacent Indonesian islands. They returned home, having enjoyed the ceremonies, meeting old friends and relatives. They were unaware of having been in contact with a fellow guest suffering from the early, most infective stage of smallpox.

The disease spreads mostly by the airborne route, but scabs from the lesions remain infective for long periods. Coughing and sneezing, with fever and malaise occurs prior to the appearance of multiple skin vesicles (Pox).

Smallpox had long been considered to be the most infectious of all the exanthema and so it proved to be. Following its incubation period of 7 to 19 days, some 100 members of the marriage party developed Smallpox.

What a clinical challenge and responsibility, what a public health hazard! Dr Rao, the Health Officer of the District took the necessary emergency measures

(1) Police surrounding the village, no one in, and especially, no one out.

(2) Vaccination of all village members who were not already infected.

(3) Water and food arrangements for the villagers.

(4)   Lotions for local application, and antibiotics for secondary infection.

(5)   Advice given regarding nursing of the sick and very toxic patients, there was plenty of help available from the many female relatives. We assisted the Health Officer in vaccinating and tracing the sick.

Before entering the village we donned long surgical gowns, caps and gloves. What a devastating spectacle, 100 people with smallpox in all its stages, vesicles, pustules, scabs. Fortunately this particular strain of smallpox carried a lesser mortality, some 5%, whereas more virulent strains have up to 40%. On returning home we entered the house via the outside door of the bathroom and locked ourselves in for the time being. We shed our tropical clothing, putting them in the bath, poured in antiseptic, mixing it well with the water. We also tossed in our shoes.

This was followed by a long shower and putting on fresh clothing. We then emerged for a much needed drink, following which we revaccinated the children, Amah, Cook, and ourselves. All had been previously vaccinated, this was a booster dose. It was effective, T.G. Of interest – the measures taken by Dr Rao were early and effective. The smallpox epidemic was kept confined to the kampong, and its members were well looked after.

The 'Emergency', as it was known with typical British understatement, was now rapidly showing its hand. It was nothing more or less than a major Communist, largely Chinese, insurrection to take over Malaya. The military weapons which had been dropped by parachute to the Chinese Communists in the jungle from 1943 to 1945, and the training in their use given by 'British Stay-Behind Parties,' for use against the Japanese, were now used against us. Spenser Chapman in his book *The Jungle is Neutral*, described well these jungle camps. In those camps he participated for nearly four years. (1943–1945). It makes most interesting reading.

Sadly the rubber planters, their staff of rubber tappers, and the tin miners bore the initial brunt. Many were killed and wounded before defensive measures could be taken. There had been rumours of something impending, but it would seem that full awareness of the true situation, and preventative measures were too little, too late.

In addition to attacks on rubber and tin personnel, railways and road bridges were sabotaged, rubber stores on estates set alight and the rubber trees slashed with parangs (jungle knives), causing their precious latex to drip wastefully away. The most vulnerable to these attacks were the Chinese and Indian vegetable gardeners living in the rural areas, growing rice and vegetables for sale to the towns.

They were terrorised by these bandits, forced to contribute rice and money, and often also their sons and daughters to the Communist cause.

If they refused they were killed, often brutally, sometimes it was 'Hobson's Choice', they were killed anyway, *pour encourager les autres*. One day on his way by car to Frazer's Hill, a pleasant hill resort, the Governor, Guerney of Malaya was ambushed and his car separated from his escorting vehicles. Bravely, the Governor stepped away to divert the bullets from his wife, seated in the car. He was shot dead but his wife was spared. His assassination shocked Malaya and accelerated counter measures.

General Templer was placed in overall command of the Emergency. A hard-headed practical and efficient soldier, just what was required, he should have been placed in charge much earlier. General Templer conducted a whirlwind but thorough tour of all groups involved, followed by the replacement of many personnel.

He developed the practical ideas of Fortress Villages and increased the numbers and efficiency of all units. The major village in an area was surrounded with barbed wire, electrical floodlighting at night, and adequate armed garrison. The vegetable growers and others were herded into this fortress at dusk, and thus protected against the terrorists. They were allowed to return to their holdings at dawn after a search at the gate for concealed rice or weapons, to ensure the terrorists were starved of them. These measures were at first resented but later largely accepted when it was found that internal committees were formed and listened to, and schools begun for their children within the fortress.

Health clinics and medical aid were also provided in situ. These measures proved very costly and for the first time personal income tax was imposed. This was to augment the tax long levied on the rubber and tin industries. Special Army jungle squads were formed, to seek and harass the Communist Groups to augment the efforts of British and Gurkha regiments already active in the field. When such a training Communist camp was discovered, usually well camouflaged, a precision low level bombing raid was often called.

Frequently the camp had emptied its occupants into the surrounding jungle just in time to avoid the bombing raid.

With regard to the many Malay kampongs, the occupants were provided with arms to defend themselves. They were not often attacked by the terrorists. Two incidents, personally encountered, may be of interest:

A young European apprentice rubber planter came to our hospital for treatment. The previous night, whilst inspecting his defences he had slipped and fallen into one of his defensive slit-trenches, hurting his chest. He had several fractured ribs, which we X-rayed and firmly strapped. As it was now past midday, on completing of this task I invited him home to lunch. Marie and I had a pleasant chat with him and saw him drive off to his rubber estate. A few days later we were so sorry to hear that he had been ambushed and killed whilst making his rounds on the estate. This brought things home to us, we felt a personal loss.

On another occasion, a Government Officer and his wife were driving from Johore Bahru to Batu Pahat just before dusk. At a bend in the road, machine gun fire shattered his windscreen and penetrated his chest. The car lurched off the road into the elephant grass, his wife pulled him clear, and dragged him out of sight into the thick grass. Luckily an army patrol, hearing the firing rushed to the scene, the soldiers scrambled out of their vehicles, and drove off the terrorists. The official, whom I knew, was weeks in hospital, first in intensive care, on the D.I. list, then further weeks in the surgical wards.

A curfew was now in force, no travelling on the roads from dusk to dawn, from town to town.

The Batu Pahat Hospital

This consisted of 150 beds, well laid out, with central admin. buildings, surrounding wards of pavilion type, and spacious grounds. An Indian Doctor was my colleague, and a European Sister was in overall nursing charge.

The operating theatre was spacious and well equipped, with Ah Peng, a senior male nurse in charge. I found him conscientious, efficient, helpful and kind to his patients. In the two and a half years I spent in Batu Pahat it was found necessary to perform Caesarian Section on six patients for Placenta Praevia (Placenta ahead of the foetal head in labour, and obstructing delivery.) The maternity ward and labour room were separated from the main block, but connected by a covered walkway, It had 20 beds, and in nursing charge was Lilian Huang, a senior Chinese Sister, who was efficient and helpful. Her husband, Bak Tee, was both senior nurse and senior clerk in the hospital administration, and was competent to administer ether anaesthetics. Overall the hospital was well equipped but post-war it lacked firm, up to date direction and guidance. This I attempted to provide.

On the maternity side I carried out Dr Lyon's methods making out lists of procedures, written briefly, clearly, and simply. Packs of swabs, bandages, binders, etc. were carefully prepared, labelled, and sterilised ready for urgent use. Instructions we given, together with demonstrations, and several dress-rehearsals were carried out.

Consistency was important, the staff appreciated a structured approach in dealing with day to day emergencies. The most common of these were retained placenta in patients brought in post-partem from the district, often in surgical shock. This condition occurred mainly in multiparous patients, those having had six or more children with, as it were, a tired uterus. The procedure we adopted was to have the patient brought straight into the labour ward, placed on the obstetric bed-table and tilted feet upwards to improve cerebral circulation, then covered lightly to conserve body warmth.

A drip saline needle was inserted in an arm vein, and transfusion begun. At the same time an injection of atropine was given, and a light ether anaesthetic started. Already scrubbed up, gloved and gowned, I would perform the removal of the retained placenta. This was immediately followed by an injection of pitocin and ergometrine to tighten up the uterus and prevent further loss of blood. The patient was carefully monitored for several hours and the lower limbs gradually lowered to normal position.

Throughout all these procedures and Caesarian operations as well, *no* blood was available for transfusion. Speed was essential to reduce loss of blood which could not be artificially replaced.

We averaged at least two such cases a month, and despite lack of blood to transfuse, we lost only one patient. In most of our patients in the maternity ward, anaemia was found on admission.

Many of these anaemic ladies were referred by Dr Marie from her women and children's clinic in the town. The remainder came in directly from the surrounding country areas. Poor diet, lack of protein, iron and vitamins, together with intestinal worm infestation and malaria were the main causal factors in production of this anaemia. Too many babies plus constant breast feeding in too short a time, could be said to be a significant factor also. In the course of correcting the dietary factors I became specially interested in the anaemia of pregnancy. Together with my Chinese Male Nurse-technician in charge of the simple laboratory, we developed a regular haematological routine, testing the blood of every maternity case admitted for delivery. Testing of the stools, for ova and larvae of round worms and ankylostoma especially, was also routinely performed. Testing for malarial parasites in the blood was routinely performed on every patient admitted to hospital. I designed a suitable needle, and with a gentle approach, and a little local anaesthetic, was allowed by the patient to perform a sternal marrow puncture. This was needed to complement the blood examination. It seemed they would not trust anyone else, but anyway I would not have delegated the task.

My microscope came in handy in examining these blood and marrow slides. It was a superior model to that of the laboratory, with higher magnification and clarity. I collected and examined over two hundred slides.

Our findings showed that the majority of these anaemia were microcytic iron deficiency in type with a few macrocytic ones from time to time.

The lowest recorded haemoglobin was 15%, the normal figure should be over 90%. This patient, some 6 months pregnant, actually walked in unaided! Her conjunctivae were a dull grey in colour. Not believing this initial finding of 15%, I personally repeated this test, twice obtaining the same result, 15% haemoglobin.

The patient was placed at rest, put on a high protein diet and regular iron and vitamin tablets. Her worm intestinal infestation was currently treated. Her haemoglobin levels monitored weekly, fast improved, with a shower of reticulocytes – new blood cells – and colour returned to her tongue and conjunctivae.

At term she went into labour and a healthy baby was born having had a normal birth. Is not nature wonderful!

A year or two later at a medical seminar in N.Q., I gave a short account of this work and my findings, demonstrating some of my slides. Many colleagues there could not accept some of the finding, especially the lady with only 15% haemoglobin and pregnant! But then they had never been abroad, nor worked overseas to see for themselves!

Many of these obstetrical emergencies occurred during the hours of darkness, and I drove from home to hospital to attend to them. The emergency was now at its height, and no one could feel safe at night outside the town. Our house was at the outskirts of the town and vulnerable. The going out wasn't so bad, but returning, sometimes hours later was nerve-racking.

The garden was surrounded by chest-high grass, an excellent ambush position, were they waiting there? As I got out of the car, Trouble, our redsetter bitch padded up, and placed her warm muzzle in my hand, saying to me, 'All is well.' What a relief!

I did not carry a firearm around the town nor at work, it was safe enough during the day. At night, however, I slept with a loaded pistol under my pillow, two hand grenades in the bedside locker, and my trusty kukri within reach under the bed. I did not want to make it too easy for them. Since I am writing this autobiography, you will surmise that they did not come.

All was not work, however, every now and again Marie and I felt the need for a change of environment and a chance to unwind and relax. We took long weekend leave, leaving my Indian colleague in charge. We drove from Batu Pahat to Johore Bahru in our Vanguard then across the Causeway to Singapore, to spend the weekend at Raffles Hotel. The early portion of our journey ran through bandit country. Marie drove at high speed, I sat beside her, pistol at the ready, and two hand grenades in the glove box. As an ex-Boy Scout, their motto, 'Be Prepared' seemed a good one to follow.

On arrival at Raffles we had a wonderful time dining and dancing, shopping and sightseeing. We returned feeling refreshed and ready for work. About halfway through our second year at Batu Pahat, Marie found she was to have a second child. As was the custom locally she continued work at the clinic for most of her pregnancy. The clinic filled multiple roles, including antenatal sessions, and had on its staff midwives of Indian, Chinese and Malay nationality who delivered patients in the town and on the district.

I looked after Marie's antenatal care and we agreed that she would be confined at home.

Ah Peng arranged oxygen and necessary medication to be at hand should it be needed. Che Sarah, Marie's most experienced, competent nurse and midwife was Marie's right hand at the clinic. Sarah was of mix parentage, and spoke English, Malay Tamil, and several Chinese Dialects. She was a gem indeed.

Our second daughter was born on March 31st 1950 at our home, Gunong Soga, after a short normal labour, and was delivered by Sarah, she was named Patricia Allyson. She weighed 8lbs 5 ozs, cried spontaneously and required no resuscitation T.G. Patricia tended to be a placid baby in contrast to Joan-Marie, but she was well aware of things happening around her. She was intelligent and thoughtful and like Joan-Marie was much loved, in the Anglo-Saxon tradition, not always shown, in contrast to the Malay and Chinese pattern of close contact.

Christmas approaching, Patricia Allyson now 8 months of age, healthy and thriving as was her sister Joan-Marie, we decided to spend our Christmas leave, not taken the previous year, at Port Dickson, a seaside town some miles north. It was thought to be a relatively safe area, and bordered on the sea. It was of interest, as having Dutch, Portuguese, as well as British influences in its history, its buildings, and its people. We arranged accommodation at a Government bungalow, then contacted my Uncle Denis, who was a scientist at the Rubber Research Institute at Kuala Lumpur to join us for Christmas.

Denis had been in Malaya pre-war. As a research scientist he

Batu Pahat. Staff of Batu Pahat Hospital and Women and Childrens' Clinic.

was striving for better yields from rubber trees and developing preventative measures against the diseases associated with them. At the outbreak of war, he joined the local territorial force and was later captured by the Japanese, and became a prisoner of war. He spent four years in this situation, first at Changi and later on the infamous Siam-Burma Railway. He survived, so many did not, and after treatment, and rehabilitation, he returned to his former post at the Rubber Research Institute, Kuala Lumpur.

At Batu Pahat we loaded our car, a comfortable Vanguard and Marie and I, our children and Amah set off for Port Dickson. We left our home and dog Trouble in the care of our cook-boy. He looked after both well for the fortnight we were away.

We made good progress, but not far from our destination we took a wrong turn and found ourselves driving through a rubber estate. Not considered the safest thing to do! We regained the correct road in due course without incident, arriving before dusk at our bungalow at Port Dickson. We were greeted by the cook-boy in charge and shown to our rooms. Amah and the children had an adjoining large room with cots and bed provided. An appetizing supper was brought to us and we settled down for the night. Next morning feeling refreshed we explored the surrounding area. The bungalow was large, with large verandah, rooms serviced by the Chinese staff and meals cooked to order. It was situated only yards from the sea, with its sandy beach. We lost no time in having a swim and paddle with the children. Denis and his wife Mary arrived a few hours later from Kuala Lumpur both looking very well. It was pleasant to relax with them, to the sound of the waves breaking on to the sand.

Next day would be Christmas Day, that evening Marie and I went to Midnight Mass held at the Catholic Church a short distance away. It was quite an experience. The church had seen several centuries pass by, it was fully peopled, the atmosphere devout and the Mass moving. The congregation was largely Asian, and sang the hymns with vigour and emotion. We returned to the bungalow, and slept well.

We enjoyed our holiday at Port Dickson, returned safely to Batu Pahat, refreshed and ready for more work. Shortly after our return from Port Dickson, a young Chinese woman was brought in to the hospital and admitted. She proved to be a co-operative patient, and an interesting clinical case, which will now be described.

A case of typhoid fever

Not so long ago, typhoid and para-typhoid fevers were common in all western countries. Safe water supplies, better sewage with positive public health measures, including prophylactic immunisation, have virtually eliminated this disease in the West. It once carried a mortality rate of 10% to 15%, not one to be lightly disregarded.

One such case, treated in our wards at Batu Pahat, may therefore be of interest. The patient was a young married Chinese woman of some 30 years of age, admitted with fever, a body rash, abdominal discomfort and distension, malaise, fever and loose stools and an enlarged spleen. Clinical examination and the clear cut history, led to a diagnosis of Typhoid Fever. The diagnosis was later confirmed by a series of blood and stool tests. The patient was carefully barrier nursed to avoid infecting the other patients. Fluids were given regularly in small amounts and carefully charted, together with intravenous therapy. Despite all available care and treatment the patient's fever continued, with frequent bowel movements and progressive loss of weight. Two weeks after her admission the patient looked close to death's door. At this time (1949), the only broad spectrum antibiotic available anywhere was Chloramphenicol (Chloromycetin), and in very short world wide supply. It was not available to us. I was aware that some might be obtained on the black market in Singapore, and made this known to the patient's husband. After much searching and at great cost, the husband managed to obtain just six capsules, of 250 mgms each. Even for one weighing only 85lbs, the patient's current weight, this dosage was less than a quarter of the minimum amount considered therapeutic. However, I felt that the patient must have built up some, but not enough, immunity over the past two to three weeks' illness. Perhaps even a little extra help might just make the difference, and pull her through. Within days she began to eat, her symptoms subsided, and she began to regain her weight. Her *joie de vivre* also started to return. Four weeks later her stools were negative to Typhoid Bacilli, she looked and felt well, and was now asking to go home!! Full instructions were given regarding diet and hygiene. The nursing staff of the ward gave her a cheer as she left for home with her delighted husband.

Again, one up for Mother Nature!!

For at least the past two years the British Government had been negotiating with its Malayan counterpart regarding the granting of independence. India had already been granted her independence, resulting in the division of the country into two major camps, India and Pakistan, Hindu and Moslem respectively.

The division occurred despite the efforts of Lord Louis Mountbatten and his team, to ensure a united India after Independence. A united India in which the parliament would consist of joint members from Hindu and Moslem groups. Sadly this was not to be.

In Malaya fortunately there was greater harmony between the main races Malay, Chinese and Indian. This afforded a less hazardous setting for the negotiations which were going on, over this post-war period. How did these negotiations for Malaya's independence affect the British ex-patriate officers? As would be expected, a feeling of unease was generally engendered. To put it bluntly, our political bureaucrats, in Malaya and Britain, were in process of easing us out. Key personnel would, of course remain, to cover the interim period, but what of the lesser souls? Already, apparent breaches of contracts were being noted, on the Government's part, between government, and ex-patriate officers – the rapid promotion of local personnel, to the disadvantage of expatriate officers being one. The trust that had long existed between government and the ex-patriate officers was being eroded. The continuing Emergency was another factor to be considered by ex-patriate officers, especially those with young wives and families. Overall, it could be said that officers over 40 years of age felt trapped in this situation, and largely decided to soldier on. Those under 40 years of age, felt that they had the option of not renewing their contracts with the Government, or of resigning and moving to more favourable climes.

After earnest discussion with my wife, I felt that the future in Malaya lay with its indigenous people. Being then only 33 years of age, we had the choice of taking our skills elsewhere. In one of the Government gazettes, I noticed that a position was available in the Seychelles Islands. It was for the post of Medical Officer-in-Charge, one skilled in Obstetrics, general medicine, Tropical Medicine, and competent in Medical Administration. In addition, a knowledge of French was desirable. You may recall, that as a boy in Mauritius, (an island similar in culture, climate, and language to the Seychelles), I was trilingual in English, French and Creole. In my final school exams in Scotland, I had passed in Higher French. It would take me only a few weeks to become fluent again in French and also in Creole, the local patois of both Mauritius and the Seychelles.

I applied for the post which appeared tailored for someone like myself. In reply, I was informed that owing to shortages of Medical Officers in Malaya I could not be spared. My application did not appear to have been forwarded by my Superior Officers to the Seychelles. This was a major disappointment to me, the post was within the Colonial Medical Service and a transfer was all that was necessary.

I loved my work in the Tropics, and wished to continue in this clinically rewarding field of medicine. In early 1951, things post-war in Britain were still austere, the people magnificent and stoic. They well understood and endured rationing, ration cards, and how to cope with the many restrictions still present.

What of Australia? Much closer, subtropical climate and stated to be welcoming medical and other professionals. Yes, Australia it would be for our 6 months' leave on full pay, and a good look around!

We said a sad farewell to our Asian Staff and friends in Batu Pahat, to our Ahma, and to our faithful watchdog Trouble. Ahma returned to her family, and Trouble we bequeathed to a dog loving ex-patriate neighbouring family. Quarantine regulations prevented us from taking her to Australia.

My wife and myself, speech at our farewell party at Batu Pahat, Malaya

Farewell Party

Our Staff and our Asian friends invited Marie and me to a farewell party, held at the Malay Club in Batu Pahat. It was a formal dinner setting with everyone in national dress, baju, kebaya, sarong, sari, pleasing to the eye in colour and style.

The evening was presided over by Dato Seth Bin Said and his wife Datin Saleha. It was a lovely evening but we felt sad at leaving so many local friends. Farewells in Malaya are always accompanied by speeches lauding the departing guests. We felt both pleased and embarrassed at Dato Seth's opening speech giving us credit for much good work. He wished us a safe and pleasant trip and hoped we would soon be back again. Several such speeches followed, in the traditional style, then it came my turn to reply.

I cannot remember exactly what I did say, but was sincere in saying how sad we were to be parting from them. During our stay in Malaya we established good relationships with all races but developed a special liking for the Malays. We found them to be a handsome, and charming people, dignified and courteous, with ready smile and laughter.

Next day we departed for Singapore and onward by ship to Australia.

CHAPTER NINETEEN

Arrival in Australia

W E EMBARKED ON THE M.V. CHARON AT SINGAPORE, a modest sized ship plying between Singapore and Western Australia. The M.V. *Charon* was primarily a cargo ship, carrying about 20 passengers comfortably, with good meals and a friendly crew. Shortly after coming aboard Joan-Marie ran about crying loudly, 'Where's my Amah'?

She was inconsolable for hours, there was little we could do by way of consolation.

'Amah has had to return to her family, they too were missing her.' To Joan-Marie it was like losing one of the family. Her distress took a long time to resolve. The M.V. *Charon* called at Derby at the southern end of King Sound, a stretch of water famous for its formidable tides. When we left the ship to walk around this frontier town (1951), the gangway sloped downwards some 45° with the ships's deck towering over us. Some hours later, after the turn of the tide, the ship was practically sitting on the muddy bottom. The gangway was now lying in a horizontal position. A tide fall of some 20 to 30 feet was the causal factor – this necessitated a continual adjustment of the ship's hawsers.

Whilst in the town, Marie and I encountered the local Medical Officer, who invited us to accompany him on his regular visit to the Leper Colony Hospital. This was situated in complete isolation some miles outside the town. He drove at some speed through the bush, there did not appear to be any obvious road. It was a hot and dusty trip. The hospital was of the pavilion type, and was run by Nursing Sisters, all of a Religious Order. They showed us their wards and patients, their records meticulously kept of each patient's daily condition. They nursed them with care and compassion. Sadly at that time, there was little effective treatment available, Oil of Choulmoogra only – not very effective, but it helped to keep hope alive. Later Sulphone was discovered which proved an effective treatment for leprosy.

We returned to *Charon* with some relief, it was hard to forget what we had just seen.

We found our two children safe and sound in the care of a good Samaritan lady who had volunteered to look after them for a few hours. She was somewhat perplexed by Joan asking in Malay, 'mau susu,' (like some milk please), as she was used to ask her Amah.

During our absence from the *Charon* some hundreds of cattle were loaded, bound for Fremantle. We heard and smelt them for the remainder of the voyage!

At Fremantle, we disembarked and took transport for Perth a few miles North, where we had booked accommodation. At the hotel, though comfortable enough, there was no room service available in 1951. Joan and Patricia needed milk, not just any milk, but milk brought to the boil, and thereby sterilised.

Armed with two bottles I ventured downstairs, and into the kitchen to obtain same. I was greeted with some astonishment by a small group of female staff, as if I were intruding into their territory. My request for some milk was turned aside, as if a mere man had no right to be there at all. Marie, on hearing my story grasped the bottles, and went down to do battle, coming back shortly with two bottles fully charged. I never found out how she did it or what transpired down there. Our plan was to spend a day in each capital city *en route* for Brisbane, namely Adelaide and Sydney. We emplaned, as the most comfortable and quickest mode of travel. Our car went on by sea to Sydney, for collection at a later date.

Adelaide in April was to us unexpectedly cold, we shivered in our tropical outfits.

Sydney was large and somewhat warmer. With two small daughters and no Amah we were restricted in our viewing. We picked up our Vanguard which by now had arrived by sea, piled in our luggage and ourselves, and with local maps to help us, drove off for Brisbane. On the way the road in parts was covered with gravel, a slippery surface. Another car passed us, not going fast, with a family aboard. Long odds but it was another Vanguard. They seemed unaware of the road surfaces, a potential hazard.

To our horror we could see their car begin to slide towards the edge, with a drop of some 20 feet beyond. It slid like a toboggan, having lost steering grip on the gravel. Over the edge it went, with a half somersault, landing stern first on its roof. We stopped and dashed to the scene, expecting the worst. Two children crawled out of the car in tears, Marie consoled them, whilst I helped Mother and Father from the car. Miraculously, no one was badly injured, but bruised, shaken, and shocked. A strong car indeed, by landing stern first, the backs of the seats cushioned their fall. It transpired that like ourselves the family were on holiday and not familiar with country driving. We arrived safely in Brisbane and took up our booking at Lennon's Hotel.

Brisbane (1951)

A clean, open air city, with a leisurely country atmosphere and casual friendly people. The trams ran right past the entrance of Lennons' Hotel in George Street.

Their sides were open in the summer for ventilation, their interior clean, their function efficient. The tram routes covered not only the city centre but extended to its far perimeters. For a few pence one could travel for miles and admire the passing scenery. The climate in April was sunny, dry, and pleasant. The City Hall, close to Lennons occupied the wide area between

Adelaide and Ann Streets. An imposing structure of hewn stone of early century design, with fluted Corinthian columns, and a high Clock Tower, which struck the hours and half hours. At this time the City Hall was the tallest city building. Alas, now it is surrounded and dwarfed by high-rise office buildings, of lesser grace.

Lennons Hotel, the best hotel in Brisbane at that time, was comfortable and welcoming to its guests. Many of the Queensland graziers, and others too, spent their holidays at Lennons, returning year after year. We were fortunate in meeting a friendly and understanding Lady Supervisor, who arranged the looking after of our young daughters, so as to allow us to accept an invitation to lunch with Dr McSweeny and his wife.

You may remember my mentioning two Australian doctors studying in Liverpool for their M.Ch. Orthopaedics, and staying at Ullet Road, with us. Dr McSweeny was one of those two. By telephone, he gave us detailed instructions to find his house. Driving with caution in a strange city, we arrived safely. On the way we could not escape noticing the many trees and shrubs which skirted the road. Many along the footpath giving shade to the passers-by, others growing in the generous gardens of the houses, creating a colourful background. Most of the houses were built of wood at this time, 1951, and stood on stilts raised about 8 feet above the ground, and with wide verandahs. This created a large area under the house, an area often concreted, where was housed the family car, lawn mower, etc. It also served as a play-area for the children and a party site for the adults, shielded from the sun, but open for cool breezes. The whole design was eminently suited to the tropical climate prevailing. Our meeting with Tony and his wife was pleasant and instructive, giving us up to date pictures of matters local and medical. Dr McSweeny had rooms at Wickham Terrace, the Harley Street of Brisbane, where he conducted his private practice. In addition, he was an Honorary Consultant at the Mater Hospital. There over the next three decades he pioneered many recent advances in Orthopaedics. He also proved to be a good friend, over the next 30 years.

Brisbane needed exploring but we were limited by how far we could take our two young children. We ventured on foot with the pram to Wickham Terrace, skirting its adjacent park, to view the Windmill, stated to be the oldest structure in the city. Built of stone blocks, hewn by the early convicts, the Windmill has endured its many years with impunity. A ferry trip across the river took the children's fancy, and gave us a further view of the city. Much has been done over recent years to beautify and utilise its twisting river banks which divide Brisbane into North and South. Four main bridges connected these two portions of the city, the Story Victoria, William Jolly and Indooroopilly, each carrying its flow of traffic. Later I called at the Medical Agency, also on Wickham Terrace, to meet and talk with its Manager, Mr Cobbold. He presented with old fashioned courtesy and charm. We discussed available medical openings, locums and practices for sale. Whilst there was no real shortage of these, none provided a family home, only accommodation for a single doctor. Prior to leaving Malaya, I had replied to an advertisement in the *A.M. Journal*, which offered a rural practice for sale, one in Western Queensland. Going with the offer, and subject to the approval of Dr Fryberg, the Director-General of Health for Queensland, was the post of Medical Superintendent of the local hospital. The post provided a new house available at modest rental. By appointment, I was interviewed by Dr Fryberg, who viewed my C.V. critically, and appointed me to the post, recommending my buying the private practice associated with it. Now to view this practice and the N/West of Queensland, of necessity by myself, whilst Marie and the children remained in Brisbane.

The first things which struck one, as it does every new visitor to Australia, are the enormous distances and the vastness of the country.

Townsville was my first destination, a mere 1200 miles North of Brisbane, some 5 hours' flight by propeller aircraft, the old faithful D.C.3 Dakota of Burma days. On arrival, I emplaned on a further flight to a country town some 250 miles west of Townsville.

A West Queensland Town
(1951–53)

THE AIRFIELD WAS A BROWN GRASS OPEN AREA, with a forlorn wind stocking guiding the direction of our landing. No buildings were to be seen. Dr X was waiting for me standing by his car, and we drove off to inspect the town, hospital and house, the town could well have come straight out of a picture book of the American West. A main unmetalled street, flanked by wooden houses and shops, constituted the town centre, together with two hotels, a Police Station, Post Office and Bank.

The weather in April was pleasantly warm by day, cooling at night sufficiently for one to reach for a blanket. Who could have guessed at the mind-bending heat experienced in the summer?

The hospital was old, wooden with wide verandahs, and was raised several feet off the ground in traditional fashion. Plans for a new hospital had long been on the drawing board, but still awaited allocation of the necessary funds.

The contrast with the Batu Pahat Hospital with its neat pavilion wards and surrounding gardens was marked. The hospital consisted of several wards totalling some 30 beds plus a 5 bed maternity ward and labour room operating theatre and quarters for Nursing Staff. A portable X-ray Unit was available for chest X-rays and fractures. At full strength the staff consisted of a Matron, several sisters and nurses, and one wardsman. (I was not to know, that come the searing heat of the summer, most of them, originally from the Southern States would fade away!)

The nearest country hospitals were 110 kms and 200 kms distant, with one doctor in each town.

Our practice population in 1951 was about 1000, with a further 500 scattered around the surrounding rural area. A total of 1500 people to be looked after medically, surgically, obstetrically.

The Doctor's House

A newly built modern bungalow with bedrooms, lounge with fireplace, kitchen, laundry and bathroom, the most pleasant sight seen so far. Surrounding the house was a wire fence with gate and path leading to the front door, and a garage to the rear. I wished that Marie could be there to look it over.

The house was built on a rise known as The Hill some half a mile from the town centre. An unmetalled road connected the two.

The Doctor's Surgery

This was situated in the main street, adjacent to the chemist's shop, a convenient arrangement for all concerned. It consisted of a fairly large waiting room, with desk for receptionist and chairs for the waiting patients.

It led into a consulting room equipped with a desk, examination couch, table, chairs, steriliser, wash basin and drug cupboard. A telephone was present in both rooms, with an outside door leading out of the Doctor's room. The surgery though spartan was functional and well situated. Dr X had booked accommodation at one of the hotels, for my stay overnight. He later took me to dinner at their house on The Hill.

We had a pleasant meal and a long chat, followed by a glass of Scotch, sitting cosily in front of the fire. We agreed on a purchase price, subject to discussing the situation with Marie, and obtaining her agreement to go so far from Brisbane. It seemed that Dr X had spent some years there, a holiday was desperately needed by them and a clear break envisaged. (After 2 years of practice there I understood how he must have felt – worn out.)

Next morning I was collected from my hotel and taken to the airfield for my return flight to Brisbane. I had several hours to ponder what I should do.

Pros and cons of the situation passed through my mind. I was keen to continue work in a hospital setting, and this offered both hospital and private practice. On the other hand the dryness and bleakness of the area, the long distances from place to place, the relative isolation was unexpected and discouraging, to a 'New Chum' at any rate! What should I do, or rather what should we do? We were on leave from the Malayan Medical Service and we had not yet burnt our boats by resigning. We could continue our holiday and enjoy and explore a new country before returning to Malaya – or, we could send in our resignation and I could take the post of Medical Super, with right of private practice. Marie would be able to take part in the work. It seemed a sensible action to take, *pied-à-terre* in a new situation and a new country. I put the whole proposition to Marie; with real reservation she agreed to give it a try. Not only that, she managed to book a cabin on the *Kanimbla*, plying between Brisbane and Townsville. The *Kanimbla* was a passenger ship with facilities to lift our car on board and store it below for the voyage. We had a comfortable four berth cabin for the three and a half days journey.

Joan-Marie was now two and a half years old, Patricia Allyson one year. We greatly missed the help of the Amah. On board we had meals in relays and many walks around the decks together, Patricia in her pram, enjoying the sunshine and the sea breezes. On arrival in Townsville, we found the weather ideal, warm and dry by day, cool at night. We stayed at the Queen's Hotel whilst making arrangements for our onward move.

We were advised by the R.A.C.Q. that the road was not one to be lightly undertaken by a young family. They recommended that they be allowed to arrange to freight our car by rail. We took their advice. We then booked seats on a flight, getting in touch with Dr X to let him know our time of arrival. He met us at the airport and took us home to The Hill.

Leaving Marie and the children with Mrs X, Dr X and I went to the hospital to meet the staff, officially as the new Superintendent of the hospital. As I would need a car pending the arrival of our Vanguard, Dr X assisted in my hiring a car from one of the two local garages.

Then to do some essential shopping to complement the food supply that Mrs X, had already placed in the fridge for us. Tired from our journey and the long day, we slept well, and on awakening ate a hearty breakfast.

Shortly after, Dr X and his wife drove up, their car loaded with suitcases, on their way south. We bade them goodbye and wished them a safe journey. We watched them drive away with mixed feelings. We were now all alone in a strange land!

The first few weeks were for us traumatic. In the domestic field, no cook-boy to prepare our meals and look after the house. No Amah to assist in looking after the children. In the professional area, as yet no receptionist to help in the surgery, and in the hospital many different procedures to be followed.

There seems to be a strong repressive element working on our memories, as defined by Dr Freud, over these early weeks. However one event stands out clearly in my memory.

At dusk during our second week, a grazier drove up to our house accompanied by his 8 year old daughter. He had driven 80 miles to bring her for consultation, because of her persistent abdominal pains and some vomiting. On examination it was clear that child had appendicitis, and required operation without delay. What a situation to be in, a strange operating theatre, no resident anaesthetist, and no trained colleague to assist at operation! Putting all these variables together, Marie and I organised things this way:

(1) Sister on duty to prepare operating theatre for an appendicectomy.

(2) Grazier-Father to act as baby sitter to our sleeping daughters, (whisky and soda provided!)

(3) This would free Marie to give the anaesthetic. Marie had 2 years' experience as anaesthetist at the Victoria Hospital Blackpool in England.

In the operating theatre, Marie had the child comfortably anaesthetized. Saying a little prayer, I commenced the operation. With care and without haste, I made the necessary abdominal incision in relation to McBirney's point, found the caecum, and traced the appendix to its attachment. Thankfully it had not ruptured, we had it in time. Routine appendicectomy was carried out, a neat closure of the incision followed, with application of sterile dressings. With the child comfortably placed in bed head and shoulders elevated, we awaited her awakening. Sleep followed soon after, her pulse and colour good. All was satisfactory, we left our patient in the care of the Sister on duty. Returning home we relieved our grazier from his baby sitting duties and reassured him that all was well, and he could have a quiet 'peep' at his sleeping daughter on his way to bed. Thus ended satisfactorily what might have been a disaster, some hours later the appendix could have burst, leading to a peritonitis, a life threatening condition.

In a small town all is known and judgement often harsh. Thank God we passed our first major test – the little girl was safely home in 10 days. Over the next few weeks we became better organised and more aware of local affairs. We managed to obtain the services of a young girl, mission trained, to help in the care of our children and our house. Amongst other things, this allowed Marie to take her own sessions at the surgery, with at first, some surprising results. In her first few surgery sessions her waiting room seemed over-filled with men, 'jackeroos' from surrounding stations, 'fettlers' from the railway, young men from the town itself. They were rather shy and in no hurry to be seen professionally, allowing others to take their place. Later, it transpired that they had never before seen a lady doctor, especially a young and attractive one. They were curious to see what she looked like! As far as we are aware, Marie was one of the first lady doctors to practise in this vast shire. It was not long before Marie became accepted in her own right by all comers. Marie and I began to learn about the local people, and their environment, work and social habits. We picked up quite a few new words, and added them to our vocabulary! There was much to learn about the local economy, the cattle and sheep stations, and small town business. In treating the ailments of the local people, such knowledge was helpful and at times essential. A few interesting and perhaps amusing vignettes are now presented to my readers:

(1) A young 'New Australian' lad was working as a member of a maintenance team on the railway line. Having finished their shift, they climbed on to their railway cart. Pumping the handles, they got up a fair speed on their way back to base. Our lad was at the front handle when he slipped and fell on to the track, the front wheel of the cart going over his chest, and the cart capsizing and throwing out the others. He was brought to the hospital with much flurry and anxiety and justly so.

Examination revealed him to be moderately shocked and shaken but in surprisingly good shape. Injuries were bruises to the chest and several fractured ribs, but no sharp edges perforating the lungs. No internal damage, a veritable miracle!

With strapping of his chest and pain relieving medication together with tender loving care from the Nurses, he was fit for discharge in two weeks. I believed it, thousands wouldn't.

(2) Sheep Dogs are an essential part of life on the sheep stations, especially one that is an exceptional performer. One such animal was brought to the surgery by its owner. A first class jumper, he had just failed to clear a high fence, and the barbed wire ripped

open his scrotum. His master was most concerned, could we do something? A splendid animal he was, fortunately, well behaved. There being no veterinary surgeon in the town, I proceeded to make friends with him. He allowed me to examine him, which I did with caution. He was lucky, scrotum ripped open but no damage to male parts. A light anaesthetic and a careful suturing was all that was required. Ten days later he returned for removal of the sutures and on departure, he licked my hand by way of a 'Thank you'.

(3) A prize milking goat was brought in by her owner, my first such encounter. We eyed each other dubiously, I was glad that she wasn't a Billy goat with horns!

The problem related to her milk bag, a mastitis or inflammation of the teats and adjacent tissues caused by invasion of organisms. A large dose of long acting penicillin was indicated. The goat's owner straddled the forepart, holding head and shoulders, whilst I attempted to give the injection, the needle bent to right angles, but did not penetrate the skin. Using a thick intramuscular needle succeeded. I had not realised how tough is the skin of a goat – one learns from experience!!

(4) Annual Race Day was a major and special event in all country towns, attended from far and wide. It is not only a series of races of local horses against each other with many bets, but a meeting of their owners and all those associated with the sport, in fact everyone.

Exchange of news, general conversation, with many glasses of beer and some local shopping make the occasion not one to be missed. Every one made an effort to dress-up for the occasion, especially the ladies, one of whom called at the surgery to fix up the family account. She was dressed as for the Melbourne Cup, large brimmed hat, necklace, brightly coloured dress, white gloves, stockings and high heeled shoes, I had met her before when she brought the children to the surgery for immunisation. She was then in her working clothes, stetson hat, long sleeved heavy shirt, jeans, and riding boots.

Virtually all the wives and daughters, as well as the menfolk, play their part in mustering of the cattle or sheep, and are expert riders.

I could not resist asking her, 'How do you do it?' knowing that she had just driven some 50 miles along a dusty corrugated road. 'Well, I'll tell you, if you keep it a secret,' she replied, and up to now I've kept it. 'It's like this,' she said, 'we drive to within 2 miles of the town and park the covered truck under a big tree. I then pour some gallons of water into a tub, and have a lovely bath. Then I change into my race meeting attire, put on my make-up, and there you are!!'

What spirit, what ingenuity, that's how the west was won!!

The morning surgery over, I drove home to pick up Marie for our afternoon at the races.

Come race number three and at the corner, the inner horse and rider were nudged against the fence. Not a smooth metal one but an old wooden one, much seasoned by scorching sun and drying winds, brittle and showing splinters in parts. One of these splinters pierced the jockey's riding boot, entering his leg. Bravely he finished the course, but was not placed! The ambulance officer drove him to the hospital alerting me on the way. Marie decided she might as well abandon the festive afternoon, and we both drove to the hospital. Quite a nasty wound, but not one to affect his later function. Marie administered the anaesthetic, I cleaned the wound and removed the wooden fragments, wound dressed, home in time for tea.

Christmas was nigh, and we were invited to join the family gathering of one of the nearby graziers (nearby 50 miles!) Summer heat was experienced during our journey in our faithful Vanguard, we arrived safely. The family home was spacious, wooden and raised in the prevailing style, with wide surrounding verandas. We were greeted by our hosts, and offered the usual drinks. Catching our glances at the numerous couches along the verandas we were told that when the party really got going some people felt the need of a quiet nap, before rejoining the revelry. The party often went on for days!

The tables were set for a beautiful Christmas luncheon for about 20 people. Just as we sat down for lunch, the telephone rang, a call from the hospital. A patient had just been admitted having a miscarriage and was haemorrhaging, would I please come right away?

With apologies, we piled into the car all deeply disappointed. Out rushed our hostess with a brace of turkey drumsticks in each hand for us. What a party to be missing!!

Our relative isolation and no relatives nor close friends led us to consider inviting my Mother and Father to join us. They were finding the British winter severe after a lifetime in the Tropics. Following several letters to and fro, Mum and Dad decided to take up our offer, arriving by air, to be met by us at the airfield.

This would be about June 1952, our winter, just the weather for them, warm and sunny by day, and cool at night. This was the first time that my parents had met our two children. It was an additional pleasure for them, also for the children.

The months flew by, Marie and I had now been practising for over 14 months on constant call, with little chance of a restful break. I had requested the Superintendent of Townsville hospital to look out for a locum for me. Eventually a locum was found. Mum and Dad offered to look after the children and the locum, who was accommodated at our house. We flew to Brisbane and stayed at the George Hotel, Lennons being fully booked.

What a relief to feel free and away from the telephone! I slept the clock round for the next 40 hours, getting meals by room service. The efforts of the cleaning lady to get in were firmly rebuffed by Marie!

On awakening we were able to take in a picture show or two and walk around the city. Our tranquillity was shattered during our second week's leave, when we read the morning paper: 'Fire destroys Chemist's and Doctor's premises in Outback town.' We immediately telephoned Mum and Dad to confirm the worst. Fortunately our Surgery had survived, the walls scorched and glass shattered adjacent to the Chemist's shop. An alleyway in between the two had saved our building. The Chemist obtained alternative premises close by and soldiered on whilst his shop was being rebuilt. Some months later Dad decided to seek an administrative post in Brisbane. Always active, he found little to do locally. Mother joined him a few months later, feeling that he needed her, especially in a strange city.

February 28 1953

A special date for us to remember, the birth of our third daughter Deirdre Katrina. As did our first two children, we were fortunate that she slept right through the night. From the very start she proved to be a warm-hearted loving child, playful, sometimes mischievous, but always helpful.

We heard that a two doctor practice in Townsville was looking for a doctor to buy out one of the partners as he intended to go to the U.K. for further studies. We corresponded, culminating in a flying return trip to view the practice and its principals.

Their surgery was well situated, appeared to be a good prospect, and Townsville a greener and more gentle situation. Now to find a doctor to replace me, most of them not too keen on practising in Outback towns. My Guardian Angel came to the rescue once more. A young Australian Doctor and his wife, a nursing Sister, were looking for such a hospital and practice, and having looked it over decided to take it on. I was glad that the people locally would continue to have a doctor.

We booked a sleeping compartment on the train, and arranged

for our car to follow us by rail at a later date. We were farewelled at the station by the Mayor and his family, a gesture we much appreciated.

CHAPTER TWENTY

Townsville

A CITY OF SOME 45,000 PEOPLE (1953), situated on the Eastern Coast of Queensland, about 1,200 miles north of Brisbane, many palms and banyan trees, and green grass lawns once again to be seen. The surgery consisted of a two storey brick building, with two surgeries and waiting rooms, a treatment room and office, all at ground level. The upper floors were occupied by a dentist and his wife, and included his dental surgery.

We were to become friends and professional colleagues, he was a competent dental surgeon to whom we could confidently refer our patients suffering from a variety of medico-dental conditions.

Our patients presented as a fair cross-section of the general population. There were also a sizeable number of maternity cases for antenatal care and delivery at the Townsville General Hospital, or at one of the local private hospitals of their choice.

On arrival we rented a house whilst looking to buy one of our own. Domiciliary visits were a significant part of the practice. We often did these calls as a family, all together. On arrival at the patient's house I would attend to the patient, whilst Marie would take the children for a walk and view the scene. On one of these home visits we spied a lovely stone house with green gardens to front and sides. Outside was a sign which stated 'House for Sale'. We lost no time in ringing the door bell, which was answered by a retired gentleman, of Scottish ancestry, who showed us around. It transpired that he and his wife had together built the house, he was an engineer. They made their own concrete blocks, cemented them in place, did all the carpentry and even dug their own well, some 20 ft. in depth! Attached to the well was an electric pump which fed the reticulation system which watered the lawns. An amazing effort on the part of two people well into their sixties.

On inspection, the inter-room doors were of red cedar and so were the built-in cupboards, the whole house was screened against flying insects, mosquitoes etc. This house was just what we were looking for and situated only a mile from the surgery. We were sad to learn that the reason for the sale was the death of his wife a few months ago. So much labour of love, a working team, and so little time to have enjoyed their home together. He was now leaving to join his son and daughter-in-law elsewhere.

The practice was busy, with much routine general work, but perhaps you might be interested in two vignettes not often encountered.

(1) A middle aged man entered the Surgery for treatment of a large, slow healing ulcer of his calf. This sort of ulcer I had seen in profusion in the post-war era in Malaya. The patient was an ex-pearl diver from Darwin, and, from his features, a classical fine Malay facies. Although his English was fluent, I could not resist addressing him in Malay.

'Berapa lama ada sakit betis kaki?' (How long have you had a sore calf of leg?)

This took him by surprise, and he appeared rather hesitant in his reply. I added rather mischievously!

'Awah sudah lupa awah punya bahasa? (Have you forgotten your own language?)

'Bukan', he replied 'No indeed.' From this point onward, we got on well in our Malay conversation and also in the successful treatment of his leg ulcer.

It made my day, it did indeed.

(2) The second vignette describes an obstetrical manoeuvre rarely performed in Australia.

It concerned a woman in labour who had had six previously

normal deliveries, and was now in her seventh. Sister I/C Ward called me to examine her, as she was having contractions but not making progress. On examination her general condition was good, not in distress, and the cervix (mouth of the womb) was fully dilated, the foetal head was high in the pelvic cavity, too high to attempt a forceps delivery.

Since no physical obstruction was found and the pelvis adequate, an internal version of the foetus would appear indicated and delivery conducted as a breech presentation. An anaesthetic was administered and an internal version performed, in conjunction with careful abdominal pressure from the assisting nurse. I turned the baby around in the womb, brought down the anterior leg, and delivered a healthy baby as a classic breech presentation with no trauma to Mother or baby.

Dicey, but I had had a first class teacher, and much experience in dealing with abnormal birth presentations in Malaya. The nurses in the Maternity Ward, called in to observe this manoeuvre, seemed duly impressed, it would be a long time before they witnessed another.

During 1953–54, the very first North Queensland Medical Conference was being organised. It would combine local clinical presentations, and also talks by visiting specialists during the day and a social evening programme to follow. I offered to present a paper and to demonstrate slides on 'Anaemias of Pregnancy in Malaya', the results of two years ongoing personal research. As mentioned in passing earlier on, some of these findings were incredibly low, so much so that some of the audience found them hard to accept, despite clear clinical facts, and demonstrations of microscopic slides of blood and bone marrow. The unbelievers have learned much better since.

Christmas was fast approaching, Marie and I thought it would be nice to invite my parents to spend Christmas with us. They flew up and we had a pleasant time together. 'My, how the children have grown!' said Mother and so they had. For some time Marie and I had been contemplating a trip to Britain and Ireland to see our respective families and friends. In addition Marie wished to study for, and obtain the Diploma in Childhealth (D.C.H.). For my part, I wished to further my operative experience in gynae-cology, and also to study for and obtain the L.M. Rotunda (Licentiate of Midwifery). But first, whom could we get to look after our patients, and what of the 'goodwill' we had paid for the practice? My partner and I discussed this situation. He had many contacts amongst the young doctors at the T.G. Hospital, some of whom were anxious to obtain a footing in General Practice. 'All right,' he said, 'I'll buy your share, and get it back from the incoming Doctor.' This was mutually acceptable, we arranged to lease our house during our absence, and booked our flight to Brisbane. Then onward by ship to the U.K. on the P. & O. Liner *Iberia*. (1955)

New adventures now lay before us, post-graduate studies, exams to sit and pass, relatives and old friends to look up.

What would the future hold for us, on our return to Queensland?

'Brisbane, beautiful one day, perfect the next.'

Que sera, sera!!

Appendix

Special Credit and Appreciation

(1) The Nagas

Acting as voluntary stretcher bearers in groups of 20 or more, in helping to carry our wounded over some impossible terrain, often at danger to themselves. They also acted as valuable sources of information as to the enemy's location, strength and movement.

(2) The Royal Artillery

They were superb in their support during the many tight corners encountered by our Infantry, following them closely through difficult terrain. Without their continual support our battalions would have faced even heavier odds.

(3) The Air Force R.A.F & U.S.A.F.

Air strikes and close support softened up the enemy resistance, destroying heavily fortified enemy bunkers and harassing their line of communication. Initially, they had fought the Japanese Air Force, and virtually destroyed their capacity to harass us. Most of all they supplied us from the air when land supply was impossible, enabling us to continue fighting.

Lastly, in the open Burma Plain they were able to carry out our wounded in a matter of hours, to safety and treatment in base areas.

(4) The Royal Engineers – British and Indian

Always at hand to help in so many ways:
   Mending damaged bridges and roads.
   Deactivating mines.
   Bridging the Chindwin and smaller rivers.
   Ensuring our water supply in the dry zone especially. Preparing
advanced airfields for immediate use etc.

(5) The Tank Corps

The hilly terrain limited their use of tanks in the Kohema Campaign. Nevertheless, tanks were winched up tracks, bulldozed for
them, to fire, point blank into Japanese bunkers, which were
resisting infantry attacks. Later in the open Burma Plain the tanks
came into their own, allowing them to give close supporting fire.
Their part in the 'Blitzkrieg' from Pokokku to Meiktila, is well
recorded.

(6) Bren Carriers and their personnel

Bren Carriers fulfilled multiple roles, scouting, attacking, supplying,
and often carrying our wounded, often under enemy fire, to safety
and treatment.

THANK YOU ALL.

(7) Nursing Service and the many other Women's Services

High praise for these ladies who served with distinction in combat
and non-combat areas in so many theatres of war. They suffered
many casualties and some endured the privations of P.O.W. Camps
in South-East Asia with fortitude.

(8) R.A.M.C. Royal Army Medical Corps.

I almost forgot to mention my own Corps., which had its personnel
at every level, from division level to R.M.O., attached to the
appropriate Army unit, (eg. R.M.O. to battalion etc. Field Am-

bulances to Brigade). Their work in the field of prevention of disease and treatment of sickness and wounded is well documented in *S.E.A.C. Souvenir of 1945*, edited by Frank Owen.

(9) The Administrative Services (R.A.S.C./R.I.A.S.C.)

Many thanks for succeeding in keeping us supplied, food, water, ammunition, etc., over an extended and increasingly difficult line of communication. They used every available and unavailable means to reach us with supplies. These means included air, rail, road, and river transport, over distances of several hundreds of miles.

(10) The mules and the donkeys

Who patiently carried heavy loads, over some terrible terrain, to supply us, incurring their own casualties from enemy fire, and falls off the steep, wet and slippery mountain tracks.

THANKS PALS.

(11) The Many Units

Not mentioned here which played their full part in the Assam-Burma campaign. Failure to mention them individually occurred because this account is one of personal experience in this campaign. Many units were operating and functioning far from my immediate area, and my ken.

THANK YOU ALL.